# OUR VANISHING FREEDOM

### The Right To Keep and Bear Arms

By

## James B. Whisker

Publisher's Development Corp., Skokie, II. 60076

Library of Congress Catalog Number 72-87869


Printed in the United States of America

# CONTENTS

# ACKNOWLEDGEMENTS

I wish to thank Dr. Franklin L. Burdette, Professor of Government and Politics at the University of Maryland for his aid and guidance in this project during which time a portion of it was offered as a doctoral dissertation under his direction. I wish to thank Mr. Alan Krug for permission to reprint and use certain materials prepared by him while he was working with the National Shooting Sports Foundation. I also thank the following persons for their criticism of the manuscript while it was in preparation: Mr. Wayne J. Thorburn, Mr. Alan Gottlieb, Mr. Bruce Eberle, Mr. James Casterline, and Mr. David Thornbury. Mr. Richard T. Brant, Jr. aided me in handling statistical material and with the graphics.

Without the aid of these friends and colleagues this project could not have been brought to fruition. The author of course accepts full responsibility for any and all errors in this book.

James B. Whisker
15 May 1972
Point Marion, Pa.

*Cover photo by Dick Friske*

For Sheila Elaine

# INTRODUCTION

As with generations past (and with generations to come) Americans of today must grapple with many serious problems which threaten to disrupt the fabric of American society. Not the least important of these pressing problems is the alarming increase in violent crime in the United States.

How we attempt to solve this problem without diminishing individual freedom is a perplexing problem with seemingly elusive solutions. As a legislator I am deeply concerned and feel that a true (if imperfect) solution can be effected only in an atmosphere of calm and rational discussion. Debate over proposed solutions must of necessity lean heavily upon the wisdom of those who drafted our American "Bill of Rights." Such debate should also train a careful eye on the history of human freedom and attempt to absorb the lessons presented therein.

I was pleased to learn that Dr. James Whisker had undertaken the formidable task of compiling a detailed history of one of man's most basic freedoms . . . the right to self protection of one's life and property, or as our Founding Fathers characterized it, "the right to keep and bear arms."

Following the style and principles of a true scholar, Dr. Whisker has prepared a documented and yet highly readable text. Furthermore, although this is a highly emotional issue, his analysis is an obvious result of logic applied to existing data. His book stands in stark contrast to the all too frequent non-rational, emotional cries of uninformed individuals who would immediately (if unintentionally) diminish this very important individual freedom.

In this age of unfortunate hysterics and irrational reaction to America's problems it is truly refreshing to come across a fact-filled, scholarly study which provides important input into an often heated debate.

It is my desire that all Americans concerned with this problem grant Dr. Whisker's study an honest hearing for it is such discussion and debate on this problem, in an atmosphere of reason, which will at the outset provide real soltuions to the problems of this generation.

Bill Archer, M.C.
Washington, D.C.
August 3, 1972

# PREFACE TO SECOND EDITION

In preparing the revisions to the second edition of this volume, I was advised by colleagues and friends within the academic profession and in the hunting and shooting fraternities to take a more impassioned look at the questions raised by those on the opposite side of the question. One eminent physician who has supported this enterprise pointed out that the principal competition to this volume has no logic, but depends on emotion, innuendo, irrationality and fear tactics. This may be true, but it is simply not my way. This volume may indeed suffer from a real emotional commitment in this way. I do not believe that a cause can be just simply because it can shout down its opposition. I believe that if our principles be right then the logic of our position should flow smoothly from this principle. Hence, we begin with our principles.

The principles involved here are simple: Limited government is best. Man is not perfectible. Just government seeks to punish only the guilty while allowing for a maximum of liberty for the honest citizen. Education and tradition are the best guides to the elimination of ignorance and to the making of just laws. Administrative agencies should not be entrusted with implied powers which give them license to prostitute the meaning of the Congress or the Constitution. The ideas of the founding fathers and the principles of history are our most reliable guides to the interpretation of the Constitution. Crimes must be punished by society, and laws already on the books should be utilized in deference to new laws which restrict the liberties of all. Crimes can never be eliminated in human societies.

These principles may mark the author as a political conservative. From this flows the probability that he will view the whole of the Constitution from a viewpoint which is sometimes called judicial restraint. Judging by recent United States Supreme Court decisions, this view has become popular once again. One may also speculate that the general population generally supports this position. Certainly, the author believes that "judicial activism" as found in the Warren Court is essentially wrong and, moreover, is quite dangerous to the public welfare.

The anti-gun forces have not been idle in the time which has elapsed since the preparation of the original manuscript for this book. The bulk of their literature shows that their arguments have grown neither in sophistication nor in logic, however. The major developments have been in the area of legislation and proposed legislation has been in regard to the so-called "Saturday night specials," the small, easily concealed handguns which are, according to the anti-guns literature, utterly without redeeming value. Bills passed have been mostly localized, but are annoying nonetheless to the legitimate shooter. The future promises more efforts in this direction.

The most dangerous trend is probably to be found in the arbitrary rule of administrative agencies whose duty it is to administer the myriad of state, local and federal laws dealing with firearms, their ownership and use. New York and New Jersey sportsmen need not be reminded of the arbitrary and controversial way the oppressive laws of these states have been administered. Those in other states need to study these laws carefully. The main results from these laws have been: enlargement of bureaucracies responsible for the enforcement; additional powers granted by implication to a handful of willful men; skyrocketing costs in administration; and, most of all, harassment of the legitimate gun owner. One shudders to think of the results of such a national law and administrative system.

The investigations for this book have led me to but one conclusion: that there was a right to keep and bear arms. It was an individual right, guaranteed to each individual citizen of this country who was of good character and mental health. Further, I came historically to associate the right to keep and bear arms with freedom and the restriction of this right with tyranny. To be sure, there is no way to say for certain that if the German people had had this right there would have been no Hitler. Conversely, I found that it was impossible to say that President John Kennedy might still be alive if we had no firearms privately owned in this country.

The scientist fears decisions made on emotion and sentiment. Rational, cool thought should be the basis for scientific investigation. Hopefully, this study was undertaken while being in the latter condition. The findings here are that anti-gun legislation cannot stand up under logic; that restrictive legislation is the result of some catastrophic event, such as the President's assassination in Dallas in 1963. In her grief America struck out at the weapon, being unable to destroy the mentality of the mind which produced this tragedy. It lashed out even more wildly as the President's murder was followed by those of Martin L. King, Jr., and Robert F. Kennedy. Its grief was unfathomable; its wisdom clouded; its revenge severe.

iv

But who bears the brunt of such legislative retribution? It is unfortunately the legitimate sportsman. It is not organized crime, not the would-be assassin, and not the criminal. Such legislation will not prevent public or private acts of passionate violence. Would that there were some way that organized crime could be controlled, that political lunatics could be quieted, and that crimes of passion could be thwarted. But it is the studied conclusion of this book that anti-gun legislation is not the key to unlock that magic door.

A way must be found to allow maximum use of firearms by the average citizen, while preventing the criminal from misusing the same sort of weapon. Penalties added on to the basic sentence for the crime which strike at the misuse of firearms is perhaps one of the best ways to attack the problem. It is essentially an untried method, but in theory at least it strikes at the heart of the problem. The proper and responsible use of our judicial system is another way. In our search for ways to protect criminal rights we might pause to study how to protect society's rights. Instead of penalizing the sportsman, we must penalize the criminal.

This study really purports to offer little new, save for the meticulous documentation of the fundamental right to bear arms. The common sense approach is simply added to academic research. If our principles are right, there must be justification for our position. From the research undertaken here, it would be this author's conclusion that our principles are right and there is ample justification for the right of the people to keep and bear arms. The book then suggests several ways in which this position can be strengthened, augmented and sustained.

Placed in another perspective, it seems a bit silly to have to justify at this late date a right so basic that it was second in consideration in our Bill of Rights. It was so basic that our colonial ancestors went to war over the denial of that right of man. Still, in contemporary society, we seemed to have placed certain "human" rights over and above this right; and we have oddly enough juxtaposed the right to keep and bear arms on the one hand and the "human" rights of man on the other. We have so broadened and expanded other rights that we have, somehow, little by little, squeezed the Second Amendment out of the Constitution in favor of these other rights.

The most basic right of man is that of acquiring and protecting property, including his own life. Without substantial means of effecting this right of self-protection, the right becomes meaningless. When society is unable or unwilling to undertake the protection of man it falls to him to do it for himself. Rising crime rates, particularly crimes against the person, such as rape, homicide and robbery, have created such a condition in our society. Additionally, with the potential of a war of unparalleled intensity and speed, a man may have to be prepared to immediately take up arms in defense of his country. The well-trained and prepared soldier has not entirely been replaced by the missile. The country must have a large reservoir of potentially skillful marksmen ready to defend it, just as the "nation of marksmen" which has existed for many centuries.

I am deeply indebted to the readers of the first edition who have been generous in their praise of the first edition and equally generous in suggestions for improvement of this book. I need to mention especially Dr. Emery Otvos, himself a dedicated sportsman and a man supreme in his own field. I have appreciated the kind support and suggestions of: Mr. E. B. Mann, Mr. Alan Gottlieb, Mr. John Snyder, Mr. Jeff Kane and, again Dr. Franklin L. Burdette. The author recognizes his ultimate responsibility for the contents of this manuscript. Errors are totally his responsibility.

James B. Whisker
Point Marion, Pa.
18 December 1973

# CHAPTER 1

## THE ORIGIN OF THE RIGHT

Perhaps because of the basic relation between arms and survival and perhaps because of the extreme dependence of men and nations on various forms of armaments few rights enjoyed by Americans have a better documented history than that of keeping and bearing arms. Plato spoke of the right and duty of keeping and knowing the use of the arms of the country and times. He advised that the citizens, once per month, "should go out *en masse*" and have tournaments involving proficiency with arms.[1] Aristotle found the relation existing between types of defense and government forms. He saw that the citizens army usually consisted of trained infantry because they could not afford the expense of cavalry, whereas the nobility of an oligarchy could afford the more expensive form of defense.[2] Rousseau,[3] Machiavelli[4] and Adam Smith[5] saw the relations between the types of army fielded in the Roman empire and the subsequent decline of the Empire when it transferred its basic army from a citizen army to a mercenary one. In the citizen army, the individual Roman had a military obligation to his state: to be prepared to defend his home and country by the use of his individually owned weapons.

The idea of the militia, that is, the principle of the citizen-soldier armed in his own home and prepared to do battle for family, king and state, originated first as one owed by the citizen, regardless of standing, to the state or to the person of the king, regardless of other ties and obligations. In the English system the principle was called *fryd*. A similiar pattern may be found in France and called there the *arriereban*. The Norman term *arriereban* was in common usage in pre-conquest days and seems to have been used last in 1758 for coastal defense purposes in the Seven Years War.[6] The principle was not a novel one when re-introduced to post-conquest England. In fact, the fryd had been used to resist the invasion of William by Harald. So important was the fryd to English military organization that one historian infers that "It is doubtful whether the military needs of the English kings could even have been met from feudal sources alone."[7] The term fryd in its medieaval context was defined as that "principle that able-bodied freemen were liable to military service

1

whether or not vassals of the king."[8] King Henry III (1216-1272) decreed that the militiamen of the fryd should possess "arms according to their (respective) possessions in land and chattels" for the defense of king and country.[9] The fryd may be defined as the "armed folkmoot of each shire" called out on behalf of the king by the sheriff of each shire. "During Saxon times in England there was a fryd or national militia service in which was one of three (medieval) duties—*trinoda necessitas*—to which each alodial proprietor was subject."[10] There was a distinction of rank made between the Great Fyrd and the Select Fryd. The select fryd were chosen for permanent duty by the citizens of districts (called hides) and were supported *in toto* by these districts. These men included naval as well as normal army personnel. The individual selected would serve a minimum of sixty days at wages quite comparable to those received by a knight of the period. Conversely, the Great Fryd, which resembles the French *arriereban*, resembles a nation in arms. It was obliged to serve only on defence and in case of emergency swelled the army regularly consisting of the royal housecarles, the regular kings' army. Quite naturally, the Select Fryd was called into service before the Great Fryd.[11] One may draw a parallel between the Select Fryd and the American National Guard; and between the Great Fryd and the citizens-in-arms principle.

The fryd obligation was in three parts. First, there was an obligation to personal service with the king, especially as summoned by him in person. In the tenth century it is recorded that the fryd "was not satisfied unless the king was there." The second of later origin was an obligation of supply service to the king or of service in the king's housecarle army without the king being present. The third was the service rendered to one's own area, whether borough or shire, under a local leader, usually the king's tax collector, the sheriff.[12]

By the sixteenth century the fryd principle in England had been largely forgotten. However, the need for men "tried, armed and weaponed, and so consequently taught and trained"[13] was felt in the 1560's and 1570's. The principle of Trained Bands was introduced c.1573 and first mention seems to be of Trained Companies, c.1576 and of Trained Bands, c.1594.[14] The government policy was to outlay money for powder, related incidentals, instructors and pay for training time and allow the Trained Bands to otherwise bear the expenses involved. The arms themselves, at least the basic tools of an infantry man, were to be borne by the individual. Mock battles and contests among the Trained Bands were quite common, expenses for which were often underwritten by the government. The firearm had come into use by this time, although the pike and bow were still quite commonly encountered. One reason for the introduction of firearms seems to have been the fact that this weapon could be more easily

2

mastered in a brief time than any other. Powder and lead were rationed severely and laws governing the private use of firearms were quite stringent outside the Trained Band practice and muster areas.[15]

The Trained Band principle, however, had many attributes of the fryd idea. There was a basic division between the Trained Bands and what one may call the "untrained bands" just as there was between the Great Fryd and the Select Fryd. For home defense the military system was based on the duty of every man to serve when the country was invaded. Men who held estates were expected to provide the cavalry whereas those of the poorer classes who were male and over sixteen were expected to serve as foot soldiers. The Trained Bands were, like the Select Fryd, select in so far as they were selected over the average citizen for this relatively intensive training. In practice one could seldom tell the difference between the trained and the untrained, so ineffective was the effect of this Trained Band training. When the Spanish Armada came, Elizabeth could count only on 130,000 men. The Trained Bands expanded this number by some 30,000 men. The untrained militia further expanded the potential defense force.[16]

The theory of the individual's right to keep and bear arms antedates by far the institutionalization of the fryd or Trained Bands. In 602 Ethelbert, King of Kent issued a proclamation limiting what was already considered a basic right of Englishmen, the right to keep and bear arms. He recognized the inherent dangers in the unlimited use of this right and therefore proclaimed that "If anyone provides a man with weapons when a quarrel has arisen . . . he is to pay six shillings compensation."[17] Eadric, also King of Kent c.650, provided in his laws that if anyone were to misuse a weapon when drinking there was to be a fine levied.[18] In the Laws of Ine (688-694) there is a provision for levying a fine on anyone who disturbs a public place by drawing his weapon.[19] The Laws of Cnut (1020-1023) provide the first written penalty in English law for interfering with an individual's right to bear arms. Statute sixty says, "If anyone illegally disarms a man, he is to compensate him . . . ."[20] In the Assize of Arms, Henry II, in 1181 not only recreated the meaning of the ancient fryd principle, but he stipulated exactly how and by whom the arms were to be borne and kept. Item two of the Assize requires that "the whole body of freemen have quilted doublets and a headpiece of iron and a lance." The only requirement was that those who "will possess these arms . . . will bear allegiance to the lord king, Henry . . . and that he will bear these arms in his service according to his order and in allegiance to the lord king and his realm."[21]

The trained Bands, although originating under Elizabeth, soon became the object of King James I's attempts to control Parliament. When

3

Charles I, on May 17, 1642, attempted to suspend the rights of Englishmen to join or participate in Trained Bands, the Parliament came to the defense of English citizens. The King issued an order "forbidding all his majesty's subjects, belonging to the Trained Bands of this kingdom to rise, march, and muster or exercise by virtue of any Order or Ordinance of one or both houses of Parliament, without the consent from his majesty"[22] the Parliament resounded with criticism of the King. It retaliated by issuing its own order upholding this time-honored English tradition, "And the lords and commons do require and command all . . . his majesty's subjects whatsoever, to muster, levy, rise, march and exercise . . . upon warrant from . . . officers of the Trained Bands."[23] The King refused to allow the militia to be supplied, and the Parliament was ordered by the King to restore the command over the Trained Bands to the King, "for the present and necessary defence of the realm . . . ." The King claimed jurisdiction over the Trained Bands according to "the Statute of Edward I, anno 1279, given at Westminster the 30th day of October."[24] The Parliament answered with a natural rights defense of the nature of the rights of Englishmen and the indivisibility of the right to keep and bear arms and to control that right. The Parliament decreed that, "no charter can be granted by the king, to create a power in any corporation over the militia of that place."[25] Both James I and Charles I had attempted, to a greater or lesser degree, to create standing armies, that of James being made of professionals and that of Charles being Irish recruits. However, the Parliament was disinterested in standing armies and quite committed to Trained Bands. The incorrectness of Charles' program can be seen from the fact that Cromwell's army was largely made up of Trained Band members particularly from London.

In 1689 William and Mary, as King and Queen, issued the English Bill of Rights. To restore the essential freedom of Englishmen to keep and bear arms, the document provided, "That the subjects which are protestants, may have arms for their defence suitable to their conditions, and as allowed by law."[26] The Bill of Rights also disallowed a standing army to be created and maintained except by permission of Parliament.[27] The obligation to bear arms for the state which had become a right accepted and recognized by Englishmen again took on the aspect of obligation to the state since the defense of the nation again for the most part fell upon the militia, since there was to be generally no regular or standing army.

The definitions of militia which emerge from this approximate period define the term in terms of both obligation and right. For example, Adam Smith defines militia as an obligation enjoyed by "either all the citizens of military age or certain number of them to join in some measure the trade of a soldier to whatever other trade or profession they may happen to carry on. Its military force is then said to consist of a militia."[28] Sir James

4

Murray, attempting to define militia in the 17th and 18th centuries calls militia "a military force, especially the body of soldiers in the service of the sovereign of a state ... (used) to denote a "citizen army" as distinguished from a body of mercenaries or professional soldiers."[29] Murray offered a second definition: "the whole body of men amenable to military service, without enlistment, whether drilled or not."[30]

The second definition of Sir James Murray approximates what has been called in international law the *levee en masse*. The Hague Convention of 1899 recognized this principle in international law and here codified it for the first time. This Convention recognized the right of the inhabitants of a territory upon the approach of the enemy to spontaneously take up arms to resist the invading troops. They were to be recognized as belligerents so long as they carried their arms openly. They were to identify themselves by an armband or similar insignia if at all possible. They are differentiated from the partisan or guerrilla warriors who have no status under international law.[31] Quincy Wright distinguishes between true militia and the *levees en masse* in this way. "Both systems may be called a "nation in arms" but whereas the first has involved a militarization of the entire population, the second has involved a civilianization of the military services." Both systems must be differentiated from the standing and permanent army.[32] Whether one wishes to agree with Professor Wright or not one must admit that both the militia as understood in 18th century England and the principle of levees en masse depend upon an armed citizenry which can rise and make use of firearms and other weapons already in their keep.

## AMERICAN ACCEPTANCE OF THE RIGHT TO BEAR ARMS

The American colonies accepted the rights and duties of Englishmen, and among these was the right to keep and bear arms. Perhaps this right was accepted over many others because of its day to day importance in the lives of the colonists who were constantly beset with problems which they could solve only by recourse to arms. The eminent scholar Charles Ellis Stevens perhaps best summed up this acceptance when he wrote, "The right to bear arms is a right involving the latent power of resistance to tyrannical government. From prehistoric days (the) right to bear arms seems to have been the badge of a Teutonic freeman, and closely associated with his political privileges."[33]

That the militia principle came to America with its first colonists can hardly be disputed. Miles Standish and the Pilgrims in Massachusetts and John Smith and his followers in Virginia seem to have organized the first real defense force, primarily to defend themselves from the native savages. Their organization seems to have been made up of a leader with some military experience, a "council" of civilian leaders who were to offer advice, and the "recruits," that is, the able-bodied men of the colony, most of whom had little to no military experience.[34] As the organizations grew more complex due to greater populations the process of recruitment became more select. For example, in 1643, the colonies of Massachusetts, New Haven, Connecticut and Plymouth formed a loose confederation for military and other purposes. The colonies were then assigned quotas of men with ratios affixed should additional men be needed. Further, following the precedent of the Assize of Arms, the Plymouth Colony had earlier passed an ordinance dated January, 1633, which required all men to own certain items of military equipment. Revisions of the law were made from time to time as suited the needs of the times, but the principle that every man was a potential soldier, and as potential soldiers must each own his own weapon and its supplies.[35] With the growing population certain difficulties were encountered in recruiting the militia. Apparently a series of harsh laws were passed by the Colony's governing body and the problem of military obligation was settled.[36]

The Massachusetts area militia was quite like the Elizabethan militia of England and the organization resembled trained bands with the richer and more prominent members of the society assuming the command positions. Conversely, on the frontiers of the Middle Atlantic states there were popular elections of officers and less distinction between officers and men.[37] In North Carolina and other Proprietary colonies the Proprietors granted to their subjects the right to keep and bear arms and in fact required this service of them. It went so far as to require service of these militia-men in other colonies or areas as required by the Proprietor or grand councils.[38] Only Pennsylvania did not raise a militia during the colonial period.

The colonials who had served in their own militia out of need soon were institutionalized into a subsidiary military organization of the Crown. The Elizabethan term "Trained Bands" was replaced with an official designation of Colonial Organized Militia. In fact, some of the King's Regulars were recruited from the militia. Other Americans were given King's commissions in American militia organizations. One of these was Lawrence Washington, brother of George Washington. These bands were activated primarily when times of trouble taxed the regulars. Others of the colonials remained inactive save for brief skirmishes in their local areas, upholding the great fryd origin of the American militia.[39]

Certain states, such as North Carolina, retained the mass militia and gave it legal standing, in addition to preserving the organized militia.

THE ORIGIN OF THE RIGHT

According to the North Carolina Militia Act of 1746, servants and the indentured caucasians were required to enter into militia service as well as freemen. Certain exceptions, similar to today's draft exemptions, were made, as for millers and ferrymen. Musters were ordered for all militiamen because of the need to prepare for such emergencies as might arise.[40]

The Indian situation seems to have had direct bearing on the militia requirements of various colonies. Virginia, which had ordered in 1632 that each man bring his gun with him regularly to church so he could exercise with it afterward,[41] required a large and broadly based militia because of its policy that all Indians *ipso facto* were hostile.[42] Plymouth Colony found it necessary to expand its militia base when it entered the King Philip's War and when it attacked the Narragansett Indians.[43] As the militia expanded so did the public law requirement concerning the great fryd militia's obligation to keep and bear arms.

By the end of the 17th century the militia system had become firmly established in the colonies. The militia consisted of mounted and foot soldiers alike, although service in the cavalry usually was restricted to those owning property of a value in excess of one hundred pounds.[44] The militias had become almost the exclusive property of the colonial legislatures. They determined that the militia was to be considered essentially civilian. Any attempts of the Royal governors to use the militia for purposes other than those expressly condoned by these legislatures were resented. This idea, already crystalized by the beginnings of the 18th century remained in face until well after the achievement of independence, and in fact this philosophy still pervades in some circles. The state governments during the revolution never changed their basic viewpoint on militia, but were forced by circumstance quite often to use militia in lieu of regular army because of the lack of regular recruits. In fact, no state ever fulfilled its quota during the revolution for regular troops, and from 1776 to 1781 militia were chosen by state legislatures to fill in the existing gaps. This practice did not evolve a consequent theory.[45] The fragmentation caused by allocating units to the regular forces proved no new problem as the militia, while trained as units, had seldom fought that way. The system had been designed primarily to train men in the use of their weapons and to militarize them to some degree, not to create fighting units which could appear at a moment's notice to do battle as a platoon, regiment, or other force.[46]

As noted above, the first clash between Colonists and British forces came about as a result of Americans' defense of their right to keep and bear arms. In the spring of 1775, General Thomas Gage had attempted to remove certain military supplies kept by the colonial militia. His first attempt to remove supplies at Salem, Massachusetts, failed. His second

7

attempt brought his troops to armed confrontation with American militia-men. Therefore the significance of the shot heard round the world may be viewed in terms of colonials defending, by force of arms, a right derived from duty, the right to keep and bear such arms as they had used to defend self and property.[47] A contemporary account describes the British purpose in this way, "By the clearest depositions relative to this trans-action, it will appear that ... a body of the king's troops, under the command of colonel (sic) Smith, were secretly landed at Cambridge, with an apparent design to take or destroy the military and other (militia) stores provided for this colony, and deposited at Concord ...."[48]

The rights of Englishmen, as understood by the colonists, involved the right to keep and bear arms. Blackstone, whose *Commentaries* were the basis for most American understanding of the law, had written that the English Bill of Rights by and large had codified the rights of men which existed prior to that time and which presumably existed into the future as well. Blackstone noted the importance of the right to bear arms in defense of one's liberty when he listed, as the final recourse of free men against tyranny, the right to use these arms. To be sure, constitutional limitations and redress of grievances by petition and court action were preferable. But the very importance of the right to keep and bear arms lies in the fact that when the legal methods are exhausted, there remains but little choice to rise up in defense of freedom. If this right were to be taken away then there would be little enforceability of rights left to the people.[49] In fact, this point of view was taken by the Tennessee Supreme Court in an 1840 case. Speaking of the excesses of power of James I of England, the Court said, "if the people had retained their arms, they would have been able, by a just and proper resistance to those oppressive measures, either to have caused the king to respect their rights, or surrender ... the government into other hands. ... If the subjects had been armed, they could have resisted the payment of excessive fines, or the infliction of illegal and cruel punishments."[50] The court is saying in effect that the liberties guaranteed in a bill of rights, in this case that of the state of Tennessee, are dependent upon, in the final analysis, the right of a free people to keep and bear arms. The Court continued in more definite terms by saying that what was meant by the Bill of Rights in England was that "being armed they may as a body rise up to defend their just rights, and compel their rulers to respect the laws." And the grievances felt by the people against the government "were for the most part of a public character, and could have been redressed only by the people rising up for their common defence, to vindicate their rights."[51]

The militia remained, during and after the revolution, an integral part of state organization. The distinctions between types of militia became greater as formalization set in, especially after the adoption of the Constitution. By 1811, all of the states had listed a total of 719,499 officers and men of the *enrolled militia*. This group was largely the creation of the Militia Act of May 8, 1792, which required the enlistment of every able-bodied white male between the ages of 18 and 44 in the militia of his state.[52] Again, this universal militia has many of the attributes of the great fryd. The Enrolled Militia were "mere lists of names and addresses of men within the statutory ages for military service."[53] This group is differentiated from the *Organized Militia* which had its origins in the middle and later part of the 19th century. This group trained in regimental size groups. "Service in the organized militia normally was considered evidence of patriotism above and beyond the normal requirement of Militia responsibility."[54] In this way one may compare it to the Select Fryd of Norman England. The *Minute Men* companies were simply part of the organized militia. The term is native neither to New England nor to the United States. It seems to have been borrowed from the Canadians where it may have originated during the French and Indian Wars.[55]

With control of the militia given to the states, perhaps as a recognition of the historic practice, the question remained whether the right should be viewed as collective through the state organization or collective through other means. Historically, the Trained Bands had owed various allegiances, although for the most part this allegiance was given to Parliament alone. A recent commentator has written that, "when a state of the union has control of a well-regulated militia, it can resist the encroachments of a tyrant or dictator." He continues by indicating that historically the dictator does not have control long if he does not control the armed forces. "The constitution," he says, "seeks to discourage one man rule by dividing control of the militia." He concludes that "the only right of bearing arms here granted is that which is done in a lawfully organized group or militia...."[56] The problems raised by this argument are several. First, what other "lawfully organized group" can exist? The court has ruled on the illegality of private Trained Bands.[57] Second, the division of militias is meaningless as a deterrent to tyranny since the Constitution allows for the nationalization of the national guard.[58] Third, the state's institutionalized national guard would hardly seem to be the type of deterrent to tyranny spoken of in the Tennessee decision cited above. Fourth, the state can hardly expect to deter tyranny within its own borders by state controlled militia. And no one would seriously expect the militia of one state to invade another state's territory to ensure a democratic government.

Perhaps a better explanation can be found in Alexander Hamilton in Federalist number 29. Hamilton says that "if circumstances should at any time oblige the government to form an army of magnitude that army can

9

never be formidable to the liberties of the people while there is a large body of citizens, little, if at all, inferior to them in discipline and the use of arms, who stand ready to defend their own rights and those of their fellow citizens."[59] Here the right is not stated in terms of the militia *per se*, but of the people collectively, although not as a whole, because of the idea of defending the rights of their fellow citizens. The Tennessee case did not set a precedent for individual action, the most likely outcome of which would be political assassination. It did not specify small groups activity which would parallel guerrilla warfare or outbursts of resentment like Shay's Rebellion or the Pennsylvania Whiskey Rebellion.

For clarification one must again turn to the interrelated idea of the *levees en masse*. Thomas Paine, chief pamphleteer for the American cause during the revolution, although most unhappy about the course of event involving the regular army had great faith in the militiaman who would leave his plow to defend his own locale. He wrote of these men, "This Continent hath at this time the largest body of armed and disciplined men of any power under Heaven; and is just arrived at that pitch of strength, in which no single colony is able to support itself, and the whole, when united, is able to do anything."[60] That is to say, the problem with the American army was its lack of desire to incorporate itself beyond the local organization which served well in times of invasion, but which had no desire to carry the war to others' areas. Functioning as such, the colonial great militia resembled the *levees en masse*. The enrollment of women in these groups given additional credence to this belief in the *levee* principle. One commentator has noted that this commitment to the risings of the citizens in general, with no distinction between sex or age categories, means ". . . that this idea of a nation in arms to preserve its liberties had already become an integral part of the paraphernalia of late eighteenth century (American) thought." He continues that "a people arising *en masse* was a 'natural' response to the English attempt to deprive the Americans of their liberties."[61] If the response of the Colonials to outside aggression or outside deprivation of their liberties was accomplished *en masse* there would be no reason to doubt that a similar response could be expected to internal tyranny. It would be unreasonable to assume that the Bill of Rights would delegate such a responsibility to the militias. One might reasonably expect that the militias might be viewed as one important training ground for the *levee en masse*. And might reasonably infer that such an uprising by the *levees in masse* would have to be underwritten by an inherent right of the people at large to keep and bear arms. It would hardly be sufficient to keep such arms in a national guard armory where they would be subject to strict supervision and even confiscation.

10

# FOOTNOTES

[1] Plato, *Laws*, vii, (New York: Pantheon, 1961).

[2] Aristotle, *Politics*, book VI, ch. 7, (New York: Everyman's Library, n.d.).

[3] Rousseau, *Discourse on Political Economy*.

[4] Niccolo Machiavelli, *The Prince*, ch. XII, (New York: Modern Library, n.d.).

[5] Adam Smith, *Wealth of Nations*, (ed. Edwin Canan; New York: Modern Library, n.d.), book V, ch. 1, pt. 1.

[6] Lee Kennett, *French Armies in the Seven Years' War*, (Durham: Duke University Press, 1967), p. 56.

[7] R.C. Smail, "Art of War" in L. Poole, (ed), *Medieaval England*, (Oxford, 1958), I, 137.

[8] Bryce Dale Lyon, *A Constitutional and Legal History of Medieaval England*, (New York: Harper, 1960), p. 161.

[9] Quoted in *Ibid.*, p. 380.

[10] Charles Ellis Stevens, *Sources of the Constitution of the United States*, (New York: Macmillan, 1894), pp. 223-24.

[11] Charles Warren Hollister, *The Military Organization of Norman England*, (Oxford: at the Clarendon Press, 1965), pp. 12-13.

[12] Michael Powicke, *Military Obligation in Medieval England*, (Oxford: at the Clarendon Press, 1962), pp. 1-25.

[13] *State Papers, Domestic Series, Elizabeth*, 12/93/18.

[14] Lindsay Boynton, *The Elizabethan Militia, 1558-1638*, (London: Routledge and Kegan Paul, 1967), p. xvii.

[15] *Ibid.*, pp. 90-125.

[16] Charles Harding Firth, *Cromwell's Army*, (New York: Barnes and Noble, 1962), pp. 4-5.

[17] Dorothy Whitelock, (ed), *English Historical Documents, c.500-1042*, (London, 1955), I, 358.

[18] *Ibid.*, I, 361.

[19] *Ibid.*, I, 379.

[20] *Ibid.*, I, 427.

[21] David C. Douglas, *English Historical Documents, 1942-1189*, (London, 1956), II, 416-417.

[22] William Cobbett, *Parliamentary History of England*, (London, 1807), II, 1354.

[23] *Ibid.*, II 1358.

[24] *Ibid.*, II, 1357.

[25] *Ibid.*, II, 1106.

[26] Danby Pickering, (ed), *Statutes at Large*, (Cambridge, 1726-1807), IX, 69.

[27]*Ibid.*, IX, 69.

[28]Adam Smith, *op. cit.*, p. 281.

[29]Sir James A.H. Murray, *A New English Dictionary on Historical Principles*, (Oxford: at the Clarendon Press, 1908), VI, 439.

[30]*Ibid.*, VI, 439.

[31]W.M. Malloy, *Treaties, Conventions, International Acts, Protocols and Agreements Between the United States and Other Powers, 1776-1937*, (Washington, 1910-1938), II, 2269; for a treatment of the principle of *levees en masse* cf. Charles G. Fenwick, *International Law*, (New York; 4th ed., 1965), pp. 665f.

[32]Quincy Wright, *A Study of War*, (Chicago; 2nd e., 1965), p. 305.

[33]Charles Ellis Stevens, *Sources of the Constitution of the United States*, (New York: Macmillan, 1894), pp. 223-24.

[34]For a general treatment cf. John W. Shy, "A New Look at Colonial Militia," *William and Mary Quarterly*, 3rd. series, XX, (1963), 175-85; for Mass. cf. Morrison Sharp, "Leadership and Democracy in the Early New England System of Defense," *American Historical Review*, L, (1945), 244-60; Douglas E. Leach, "The Military System of Plymouth Colony," *New England Quarterly*, XXIV, (1951), 342-64; also, Allen French, "The Arms and Training of Our Colonizing Ancestors," *Mass. Historical Society Proceedings*, LXVII, (1941-44), 3-21.

[35]Cf., Jack S. Radebaugh, "The Militia of Colonial Massachusetts," *Military Affairs*, XVIII, (1954), pp. 1-18; also, Leach, *op. cit.*, esp. pp. 351ff.

[36]Cf. Leach, *op. cit.*, 353ff.

[37]Cf., Sharp, *op. cit.*

[38]E. Milton Wheeler, "Development and Organization of the North Carolina Militia," *North Carolina Historical Review*, XLI, (1964), 307-23.

[39]Jim Dan Hill, *The Minute Man in War and Peace*, (Harrisburg: Stackpole, 1963), p. 4.

[40]Wheeler, *op. cit.*, pp. 312-13.

[41]William Waller Hening, (ed), *Statutes at Large*, (Richmond, 1810-23), I, 174.

[42]Shy, *op. cit.*, p. 177.

[43]Leach, *op. cit.*, pp. 358ff.

[44]Louis Morton, "The Origins of American Military Policy," *Military Affairs*, XXII, (1958), pp. 74-82.

[45]Hugh Jameson, "Subsistence for Middle States Militia, 1776-1781," *Military Affairs*, XXX, (1966), 121-134; for additional treatment of the civilian nature of the militia and its subjugation to state legislatures, cf. E.J. Fisher, *New Jersey as a Royal Province*, (New York: Columbia University, 1911); N.D. Merenes, *Maryland as a Proprietary Province*, (New York, 1901), and Herbert Levi Osgood, *The American Colonies in the Eighteenth Century*, (Gloucester, Mass.: Peter Smith, 1958), esped. II, 210-11.

[46]Morton, *op. cit.*, p. 80.

[47]For treatment of background to this event, cf. Bernhsrd Knollenberg, *Origin of the American Revolution, 1759-1776* (N.Y., 1960), and John Shy, *Toward Lexington*, (Princeton, 1965), For the event per se, few accounts surpass Christopher Ward's, *The War of the Revolution*, (New York, 1957), 2 vols.

[48]"Address by the Massachusetts Provicial Congress, sitting at Watertown," to "The Inhabitants of Great Britain," April 26, 1775 in Alden T. Vaghan, (ed), *Chronicles of the American Revolution*, N.Y.: Grosset and Dunlap, 1965), pp. 167-68.

[49]Blackstone's *Commentaries*, I, 143-44.

[50]*Aymette v. the State*, 2 Humphreys 154.

[51]*Ibid.*

[52]Russell Frank Weigley, *History of the United States Army*, (New York: Macmillan, 1967), pp. 93-94.

[53]Hill, *op. cit.*, p. 28.

[54]*Ibid.*, p. 26.

[55]*Ibid.*, pp. 28-29.

[56]J.A. Richard, et. al., *Our National Constitution: Origins, Developments, Meaning*, (Harrisburg: Stackpole, 1955), pp. 235-36.

[57]*Presser v. Illinois*, 116 U.S. 252.

[58]Art. I, sec. 8, col. 12.

[59]Alexander Hamilton, "Federalist Number 29," *Federalist Papers*, (New York: Modern Library, 1937).

[60]Thomas Paine, "Common Sense" in *Collected Works of Tom Paine*, (New York: Modern Library, 1937, p. 31).

[61]Orville T. Murphy, "The American Revolutionary Army and the Concept of *Levee en Masse*," *Military Affairs*, XXIII, (1959), pp. 13-20.

# CHAPTER 2

## THE CONSTITUTIONAL RIGHT TO BEAR ARMS

While the body of the United States Constitution did not specifically sanction the *right* to bear arms, the federal government, soon after the ratification of the basic document, found sufficient authority to require of each able-bodied man between eighteen and forty-five the *obligation* to keep and bear arms for defense of the state. Each free, white, able-bodied male was required by the Militia Act of May 8, 1792 to furnish for his individual use "a good musket or firelock" with appropriate equipment and ammunitition.[1] As in Europe in earlier days, the citizen has been required to keep and bear arms; this obligation was soon to be viewed by citizens as a right and by the government as a questionable privilege for the individual and a collective right only for the militia under the Second Amendment. The "great militia" as defined by the 1792 Militia Act still exists at least in theory. It has been subsequently enacted into such bills as the Militia Act of 1862, the Militia Act of 1903 (called the Dick Act), and the Volunteer Act of 1914.

## THE ORIGIN OF THE BILL OF RIGHTS

It has now been well over a century and a half since the second amendment to the United States Constitution was added to the body of that document. While it is nearly impossible to project the precise reasoning for that amendment and to determine exactly what the framers meant by it, it is possible to say certain things about that amendment with a certain degree of certainty. The body of the Constitution contains a good statement of the rights and powers of that state militias (national guard units). It would be futile to state that the framers had nothing more in mind than a reaffirmation of the right already in existence and thoroughly guaranteed previously. The rights considered in the Bill of Rights are clearly grants of power to the individual citizen for the most part. Such has been the interpretation of the United States Supreme Court, quite rationally and logically, in virtually every case when it has been called upon to interpret the words of the Bill of Rights.

15

The framers of the Constitution, according to the extant reports, spent very little time considering the bill of rights. They had been prompted to begin work on a new fundamental document for government. Alexander Hamilton had acted as spokesman for many before the Constitutional Convention in Philadelphia when he drew up his list of weaknesses of government under the Articles of Confederation. The government was broke; there was no other way to say it. And, worse yet, he saw that the colonies now independent of British rule for a decade had failed to develop responsible government. A strong fear of central power and of the executive office in particular had caused the colonists to create an impotent, weak, disunited meeting forum type of central "government." Foreign and domestic pressures mitigated against the success of so weak a system. Taxing power and control over interstate commerce were denied to the central administration. These were the major crises to be faced in Philadelphia.

Virtually no one concerned himself directly with the questions concerning the maintenance of the newly won "rights of Americans" at the long sessions at Carpenter's Hall. However, toward the latter days of the Convention, George Mason of Virginia spoke concerning individual rights. "The Constitution," Mason said, "should be prefaced by a Bill of Rights. It will give great quiet to the people." Elbridge Gerry of Massachusetts then placed a motion on the floor which would have created a committee to prepare such a statement of fundamental rights. However, much opposition appeared led by Roger Sherman of Connecticut. Sherman maintained that such a Bill of Rights was unnecessary and superfluous. The motion of Gerry was then defeated.

The Anti-federalist camp, however, used this failure by the convention as one of its principal objections to the newly proposed Constitution. While there was no concensus as to what should have been included in such a Bill of Rights, there was much agreement that there should have been *some* such enumeration of rights. Thomas Jefferson in a letter sent from Paris to James Madison, then one of the strongest Federalists and one of the authors of the *Federalist Papers*, spoke of this matter. The Constitution, Jefferson wrote, "is a good canvas on which some strokes only want retouching. What these are, I think, are sufficiently manifested by the general voice from North to South, which calls for a Bill of Rights."

Alexander Hamilton felt that the power to abridge civil liberties simply did not exist. He felt that to pass such laws a clear grant of power would have to have been given to the national legislature under the new constitution. Clearly, Hamilton, while a federalist, was not in favor of extreme centralized power. He felt that what may be best described as a balanced centrist system was in the final analysis the best guarantee of human liberties. To place one's trust in documents and laws is to run the risk of losing these rights entirely. Put another way, Hamilton foresaw the probability that the Constitution would be interpreted, reinterpreted, and even misinterpreted by future generations in all branches of government and even ignored by some governors so that in the final analysis the good practice of government by men of good will and learning is the single protection from tyranny. He had witnessed the prostitution of rights by the English government, both in the colonies and at home, despite the existence of such guarantees as the English Bill of Rights. After all, it was for the existing Rights of Englishmen that the colonists had rebelled.

John Hancock found the best political device to guarantee the addition of a Bill of Rights to the body of the Constitution. Hancock proposed to the Massachusetts ratification convention that its ratification of the Constitution be conditional. The convention then made its acceptance dependent upon the addition of a Bill of Rights, and a few other states then followed suit.

James Madison, as one of the first orders of business in the first congress of the United States under the new Constitution then proposed meeting this obligation. Madison drafted twelve articles of which ten were ratified by the states in short order. The right to keep and bear arms had not been proposed second in order, but so widespread was its acceptance, and so little question existed in the colonial mind as to its necessity that it was second to be ratified by the states. Only the guarantees of assembly, association, religion, free speech and press were considered first. It was given precedence over rights against excessive governmental powers such as cruel and unusual punishment and the quartering of troops in private homes.

## THE RIGHT TO KEEP AND BEAR ARMS

The second amendment to the American constitution has been called the "lost amendment" by its most recent historian.[2] It would seem that an article guaranteeing a basic liberty written into the country's basic document as its second major addendeum would be somewhat differently considered in an age when the basic civil liberties and rights of the people are being so closely considered by the bulk of its population. However, the fact remains that the United States Supreme Court has not reviewed a single case of basic nature concerning this right in the last decade. It is also true that the right to keep and bear arms has not been the subject of major public law treatment. There seems to be no clear cut understanding of the intent of the Founding Fathers in regard to the Bill of Rights *in toto* to say nothing of the second amendment alone. If the purpose of the Fathers was in fact to state the basic rights of free men, rather than simply enumerating certain beliefs about the nature of limited government, then it is essential to understand how the right of free men to bear and keep arms affects the citizen today.

The second amendment was drafted by James Madison and read, as introduced in the first Congress, "The right of people to keep and bear arms shall not be infringed; a well armed and well regulated militia being the best security of a free country: but no person religiously scrupulous of bearing arms shall be compelled to render military service in person."[3] However, Elbridge Gerry immediately objected that those in power "can declare who are those religiously scrupulous and prevent them from bearing arms."[4] The amendment proposed then was altered to read, as it stands today, "A well regulated militia being necessary to the security of a free state, the right of the people to keep and bear arms shall not be infringed."[5]

The right also appeared in period state constitution, although the distinction was seldom made between a collective right and the individual right, the basic language being either "the right of the people" or "the right of the citizen."

The right to bear arms was considered to be a basic right, secure against colonial government and English King, and the Constitutional guarantee seems to have been taken in large from at least six earlier state constitutions: Massachusetts, Vermont, Virginia, North Carolina, New York and Pennsylvania.[6] The American Revolution by and large seems to have had as its proximate cause, regardless of one's views of remote causes, the violation of the right of the colonials to keep and bear arms. In fact, the Battle of Lexington, April 19, 1775, was brought about by the resistance of the continentals to British who were attempting to seize their powder and other gun-related supplies.[7] This attempt to limit the right of keeping and bearing arms was listed in the Declaration of the Causes of Necessity of Taking Up Arms, dated July 6, 1775, as one of the reasons of the American Revolution.[8] It would therefore seem natural that the right abused by the British administration should have been protected in contemporary charters.

The state constitutions expressly guaranteed that the right ought not to be abridged by the state governments. Virginia's Constitution of 1776 guarantees in Section XIII this right and defines the militia having the right to keep and bear arms as being "composed of the body of the people, trained to arms."[9] Pennsylvania in its 1776 Constitution declared that "the people have a right to bear arms for defence of themselves and the state" in its Article XIII.[10] North Carolina's 1776 Constitution provided only for the "defense of the state"[11] while Vermont followed the Virginian inclusion of self-defense.[12] Massachusetts spoke of the "collective defense" in its 1780 Constitution.[13] New Hampshire,[14] Maryland,[15] and Delaware[16] speak in the colonial constitutions only of the function of the militia and its being "proper" and "the natural defence of free government."

The second amendment, like all parts of the Bill of Rights, was interpreted first as a prohibition operative only upon the federal government. In the historic case of *Barron v. Baltimore*[17] in 1833 the Supreme Court upheld this contention. This philosophy still pervaded in the two later cases of *United States v. Cruikshank*[18] in 1876 and *Presser v. Illinois*[19] in 1886. However, in a landmark case in 1925, *Gitlow v. New York*, the United States Supreme Court reversed its earlier position, and began to incorporate the Bill of Rights provisions vis a vis the state governments encroachments on individual rights. While the case involved only the freedom of press and speech,[20] the Court had in fact opened the floodgates that have subsequently allowed other Bill of Rights freedoms to come under the due process clause of the fourteenth amendment. In 1937 in the case of *Palko v. Connecticut*, Justice Benjamin N. Cardozo set the criteria to determine if a state has violated the rights of individuals protected by the fourteenth amendment. Cardozo indicated that freedom of speech, press, religion, assembly and most items concerned with speedy and just trial were included in this protection because they were essential to liberty. He indicated that the Court in the future ought to consider which rights were "implicit in the concept of ordered liberty" and which are "so rooted in the traditions and conscience of our people as to be ranked as fundamental" or if denied to individuals the act would be "shocking to the sense of justice of the civilized world."[21] The Cardozo criteria is therefore quite arbitrary and individual value-oriented. How the second amendment fits within the established criteria has yet to be determined because of this failure of the Court to date to state either that the right to keep and bear arms is or is not so conceived to be fundamental to an ordered concept of liberty, justice and human rights.

Proponents of control bills find that certain disadvantages accrue from private ownership and use of firearms, such as availability of firearms to the criminal element, youths and mentally derranged. This would seem to necessitate advocacy of the form of prior restraint contained in the Minnesota public law in regard to the press which was overturned in the case of *Near v. Minnesota*[22] by the Supreme Court in 1931. In this case the court ruled that a state cannot prohibit publication of a paper which has had a prior history of law violations. Instead of enjoining an individual from publishing the state may exercise its police power only in criminal actions against individual violations of the law.

19

Whether the *Near* principle can be applied to restraints on the exercise of the right to keep and bear arms has yet to be determined by the Court. However, the advocates of firearms control legislation seem to tend toward some form of prior restraint as the preferential way of handling the problem.

The fact remains that the rifleman in modern warfare is not obsolete and therefore must be trained. The value of a reserve of riflemen previously trained in the use of firearms can be stated in various ways and with various degrees of intensity, yet there still is some admitted value granted by all discussants. The right of self-defense, through firearms as well as other means, seems to be quite as important today as in any period of American history. How these advantages can be weighted to balance the obvious disadvantages inherent in the right to keep and bear arms must be eventually made by the Court.

# THE SUPREME COURT RULES ON FIREARMS

The United States Supreme Court has dealt very little with the right to keep and bear arms. It has ruled on the second amendment only five times in its history. Four of these five rulings were made in the nineteenth century, and the latest court ruling was made in 1939. It would seem that the Court must soon deal with this amendment. In reality, the Court made little attempt in any of its five previous rulings to define what rights are guaranteed by the Second Amendment. The Court was primarily interested only in the operations of the state legislatures in the field of firearms control. All five Supreme Court cases dealt with firearms exclusively, hence it is logical to assume that the Court is interested only in controls and rights involving the right to keep and bear *fire*arms.

In the first case[23] handled by the Court involving the Second Amendment the Court was interested primarily in a state law which restricted the right to keep and bear arms within the territory of a specific state. The basic ruling of the court held that the right of the people to keep and bear arms was not guaranteed in the Constitution but that it also was not dependent upon that instrument for its existence. The Court held that the right to keep and bear arms as set down in the Bill of Rights meant nothing more than this right shall not be infringed by the federal government. The case was primarily concerned with the constitutionality of a federal law[24] which attempted to legislate federal policing of abridgments of the newly obtained Negro civil rights. Generally, the right of the federal government to enter into any form of local policing was reserved to the states and forbidden to the federal government; and such prohibited policing included the interference with the right to bear arms by the federal government.[25]

The second ruling[26] by the Court was more concerned directly with the second amendment and was decided entirely with reference to the right to keep and bear arms. An Illinois citizen named Herman Presser had been convicted under an Illinois state law which prohibited uniformed private military or para-military groups from bearing arms publicly. Presser's group, the *Lehr und Wehr Verein,* marched in Chicago on September 24, 1879 with about 400 members, all armed with rifles. The Court again accepted the view that the Second Amendment was a limitation only on the federal government and represented no protection for the citizen against encroachment by the states. The Court said, "This is one of the Amendments that has no other effect than to restrict the powers of the National government, leaving the people to look for their protection against any violations by their fellow-citizen . . ." to their own state constitutions.

The Court did hold that since it is "undoubtedly true" that all citizens, regardless of age or sex, "constitute the reserved military force or reserve militia of the United States." In effect, the Court recognized that there was a *levee en masse* or "great militia" in the United States. In view of this principle the Court rules that ". . . the states cannot, even laying the constitutional provision in question out of view, prohibit the people from keeping and bearing arms, so as to deprive the United States of their rightful resource . . ." for the army and the militia. To do this would be to "disable the people from performing their duty to the general government." On the operative level the Court seemed to be unable to decide how this basic right (and obligation) should be preserved. It held that the government of the United States "can neither grant nor secure to its citizens any right or privilege not expressly or by implication placed under its jurisdiction." And the Court found, "All that cannot be so granted or be secured are left to the exclusive protection of the State." The Court then ruled in favor of the state law saying that it had no choice since, "The right voluntarily to associate together as a military company . . . without, or independent of an act of Congress . . . is not an attribute of national citizenship." The states were therefore found to have the right to regulate the ". . . parading of military bodies and associations, except when such bodies or associations are authorized by the militia laws of the United States."[27]

The basic premise of the two earlier cases was again upheld eight years later in a case arising out of Texas. Franklin P. Miller brought suit against the state of Texas charging the legislation restricting the carrying of dangerous weapons was unconstitutional. Miller claimed protection under the Fourth and Second Amendments. The Court held that the restrictions

21

contained in the Bill of Rights were operative only on the federal government. Further, it held that "The statute of Texas prohibiting the carrying of dangerous weapons does not abridge the constitutional privileges or immunities of citizens of the United States."[28] This decision has subsequently tacitly underwritten the right and power of the state, operating under its reserved police powers, to control dangerous weapons within its state boundaries, limited only by the provisions of its state constitution subject to state judicial review.[29]

In 1939, the Court took an in-depth look at the Second Amendment. The Congress has passed the National Firearms Act, a revenue act aimed at licensing and controlling certain weapons in interstate commerce. The conviction of several parties for the possession of an unlicensed weapon, a shotgun with a barrel less than eighteen inches, led to the Court's consideration in May 1939. The Court traced the history of the right and obligation to bear arms for the defense of the state, from pre-Norman days through the writings of learned scholars and the constitutional period of American history. The Court concluded from its historical analysis that ". . . from the debates in the [Federal] convention, the history and legislation of Colonies and States, and the writings of approved commentations . . ." it is possible for one to ". . . show plainly enough that the Militia comprised all males physically capable of acting in concert for the common defense." It noted that ". . . when called for service, these men were expected to appear bearing arms supplied by themselves and of the kind in common use at the time." The Court accepted Adam Smith's definition of militia which said in essence that a militia was comprised of non-professional soldiers whose primary profession was dominant over that of soldiering. It held then that there was a right inherent in all of American history to bear arms and suitable ammunition for self and the common defense, but the Court was unable to link this right with that supposed right which was supposedly violated by the act in question. The court's finding then was that "In the absence of any evidence tending to show that . . . [the weapon in question] has some reasonable relationship to the preservation of a well regulated militia . . ." it is impossible to say that the Second Amendment guarantees any right to keep and bear such a device. The Court referred to a Tennessee decision, *Aymette v. State*, in support of its attempt to define, by the process of exclusion, what weapons are covered by a constitutional right to keep and bear arms.[30] The Court primarily was concerned with protecting the right of the people to keep and bear arms whose ". . . use could contribute to the common defense." The Court notes that the right guaranteed by the Second Amendment was concerned with the right of individuals to keep and bear arms in accordance with the principle which the Court had found in history, that if

22

the average citizen-soldier who could be rapidly enlisted in the unorganized militia using his personal weapons. "With obvious purpose to assure the continuation and render possible the effectiveness of such forces the declaration and guarantee of the Second Amendment were made. It must be interpreted and applied with that end in view."[31]

The *Miller* decision is noteworthy because it is the first and only in-depth coverage of the Second Amendment by the U.S. Supreme Court. However, The Court dealt only with the constitutionality of the one Congressional act. The disposition of the state controls essentially remained the same as the earlier Court decisions. The recognition of the necessity of having a well-regulated citizen-army reserve is very much at the heart and soul of this court decision. The groundwork was most certainly laid for a future decision which could uphold the right of the private citizen to keep and bear arms against any state encroachment. This could be done under two separate lines of reasoning: the one could invoke the obligation of the citizen to be armed for defense of state and nation; and the other could invoke the right of the citizen to be armed for a variety of reasons, including his right to be prepared to resist assault or tyranny.

The National Firearms Act has subsequently been invalidated in part in two separate Court decisions, but this invalidation has taken place under the Fifth Amendment's right against self-incrimination and not under the protection of any part of the Second Amendment. The Court struck down the registration requirement of this act because "It is apparent that regis-tration . . . would be an admission that another section or other sections of the Act had been violated and might support a conviction by the Court."[32] However, the other sections of this law are still valid, and no protection has been offered by the Court under the Second Amendment.

The court philosophy inherent in the cases before 1925 was that no part of the Bill of Rights including the Second Amendment was included under the "due process" clause of the Fourteenth Amendment, and there-fore the petitioner from the state court had no recourse to the federal courts for Bill of Rights liberties and guarantees.[33] However, a landmark decision in 1925, *Gitlow v. New York*, brought the freedoms on speech and press of the First Amendment under the protection of the Fourteenth Amendment vis-a-vis the state government's infringements of these rights.[34] The net effect of this decision and other similar decisions has been to bring about an ever increasing involvement of the federal government in the protection of the people against abuse of their fundamental liberties by the states.

Thus far virtually all parts of the Bill of Rights which have come up for review have eventually been accepted under the protection of the "due process" clause. This includes the Ninth Amendment which formerly had

23

been almost entirely dormant.[25] This is worthy of note here primarily because it is possible that the right to bear and keep arms may be protected, if not elsewhere, under the Ninth Amendment. The *Presser* decision noted that even laying this provision of the Second Amendment aside, the states cannot prohibit the people from keeping and bearing arms. Such a protection may be found in a combination of the Second and Ninth Amendments, as included under the Fourteenth Amendment. Presumably, the Ninth Amendment being indefinite as to specific rights to be protected, here again there is room for the court operation of judicial inclusion and exclusion.[36]

Another possible approach to constitutional protection of the right to keep and bear arms is to be found by analogous extrapolation from the freedom of the press principle in *Near v. Minnesota*. In this case the Court held that a state cannot enjoin a publication from publishing permanently. Such an injunction would rob the people of the news and interpretation of the news from a point of view. A publication may be prosecuted for violations of the law, as in libel or slander. In this case the Supreme Court voided as unconstitutional a state law which authorized public officials to forbid publication of "malicious, scandalous and defamatory" newspapers.[37] This was an extension of the Fourteenth Amendment. By analogy, the Court might assume that the obstacles to keeping and bearing arms set up by repressive state laws, such as New York's Sullivan Law, which required proof of need of a firearm before a purchase or ownership permit is issued, might be a form of "prior censorship" or "prior restraint" in violation of the due process clause of the Fourteenth Amendment. It might further assume that these obstacles represent a form of permanent restraint placed by the states upon the national obligation of citizens to be prepared to form one of the various forms of popular resistance to an enemy in times of war, whether as citizen-soldier, member of the "great and unorganized militia" or as part of the *levees en masse*.

In general, then, it must be assumed that the Second Amendment represents one of the very few Bill of Rights guarantees that has not been applied to the states, but that it also might be so applied at any time under any one of a number of possible avenues of approach by the Supreme Court. It also must be concluded that with the passage of more than four decades since the original incorporation decision in 1925 there is a general obligation upon the Court to hear a trial case in order to reconcile misunderstandings on this amendment. However, an adverse decision need not end all hope of incorporation, as the Court has many times in the past reversed itself.

A general conclusion, especially in view of the Miller decision is that there is somewhere some right to keep and bear arms. And one is inclined to believe the question is far from being at rest as more and more legislation is passed by state legislatures, to say nothing of legislation being considered by the Congress. Since the *Presser* decision excluded from consideration private military or paramilitary groups, it is to be presumed that this type of keeping and bearing of arms in not to be considered. The study of the minute-man types in the Miller decision, and the hint in this direction in the *Presser* decision, would leave one to the conclusion that eventually a Supreme Court decision much along the lines of the cited *Aymette v. State* decision in the Tennessee state courts will try to discern what types of arms are to be considered as protectable from state restriction. This type may be nothing more than the ordinary rifle or/and pistol used by the army and/or state National Guards, or it may include various other forms of weapons.

If the ordinary weapons used at the time by the armed services be the criteria, then the Court will be forced to take a stand again on the National Firearms Act, and perhaps make minute distinctions under this law, since the prevailing weapons are generally capable of fully automatic fire.

If the Courts were to decide that the types of weapons that protected are the military calibre or types of weapons, then it might be useful to model Switzerland whose public law requires that each adult male, after undergoing their universal military training, is required to keep in his home the prevailing military weapon ready for use in defense of self and nation. Such a requirement would be but a small addition to the prevailing public law, as found in the US Code; and it would be in keeping with US tradition, as in the early Militia Acts. Such a group would form not only a nucleus for an army in a national emergency, but also in case of internal disruptions. The supply problems inherent in calling up large numbers of men would also be partially eliminated if each citizen-soldier had his own weapon and at least a minimal supply of ammunition for it. Again, this philsosophy has in part been adopted in the Civilian Marksmanship Program sponsored in part by the Director of Civilian Marksmanship, and subsidized in part by the federal government. Such projects have, in the past, been underwritten by the releasing at minimal cost to the purchaser obsolescent military weapons.

## CONCLUSIONS

Great emphasis has been placed on a vast number of rights which are the property of all Americans; and this emphasis is of course quite correct. As this manuscript is being prepared, many Americans are celebrating the

25

victory of the free press over government censorship in the New York *Times*—Washington *Post* publication of the so-called "Pentagon Papers." Civil libertarians have recently spoken with pride of the victory which was won over regulation of hard-core pornography. In short, all of the first amendment rights have found strong and virtually unlimited support in recent court decisions. We truly have established a libertarian society with respect to almost all of the Bill of Rights. With this support of freedom we agree. We do not choose to disparage the enforcement of any right. It is, in fact, in this same spirit that we approach the neglected portion of the enumerated rights of the Bill of Rights.

The purpose of the Bill of Rights was to remove from the popular will the possibility of curtailing certain basic rights. The document was written against a strong natural rights background. Men, the Founding Fathers believed, "were endowed by their Creator with certain inalienable rights." It is worthwhile to break down this oft-quoted claused aphorism of John Locke into its component parts. "Certain" means that it is possible, by human thought and reflection, to enumerate or list specifically what these rights are. "Inalienable" means that they are a portion of the basic nature of man. To curtail these rights would make man a moral cripple. "Endowed by their Creator" means that these are God-given rights with which man may not legitimately tamper.

The Founding Fathers noted that there were some rights which men had, but which they did not enumerate. To protect these rights equally the Ninth Amendment was written. It holds that the enumeration of rights (in the first eight amendments) is neither complete nor definitive. Among the rights one might legitimately include here would be that of self-defense.

Among those right enumerated in Amendments I through VIII only the Second gives a reason for its existence. It holds that "a well-regulated militia" is "necessary for the common defense" and therefore it is necessary to ensure this right to the "people." As we shall see, however, this is not the only legitimate reason for keeping and bearing arms. There are many such reasons; however, it should be necessary to find only one substantial reason to maintain the right. However, when attempting to abridge any right the burden is overwhelmingly on government to demonstrate clearly and beyond any doubt that such a right must be removed.

Powers granted to government, whether do act negatively or positively, originated with the people, not with the government. The government is by its very nature a *compact*. It has been an academic question whether the compact involved the states, the people of the states or the people as a whole. If the first argument be accepted, the people are then viewed as having formed state governments. The people, however, are ultimately sovereign. The sovereignty granted by the people is limited in scope and nature, and the power to usurp the rights of the people is not included among government's delegated powers.

When the Constitution of the United States was presented to the states for ratification many objections were voiced concerning the lack of guarantees of basic rights. James Madison then undertook preparation of a series of proposals which resulted in our Bill of Rights. Ratification was secured only after the promise of this vital document. Madison, true to his word, introduced a series of amendments into the very first session of the Congress. The right to keep and bear arms appears as the second article of this provision of human liberty.

In recent years, the federal government has undertaken the protection of virtually all of these enumerated rights—except for the Second Amendment rights. Originally, the Bill of Rights was viewed by the courts as a limitation on the federal government only. It did not limit state encroachments of these same rights. In essence, if a state sought to abridge any individual right, the individual had to appeal to the state courts in his state of residence for protection. If that state's constitution offered no protection the individual suffered the loss of that right. This trend continued through the second decade of this century until in *Gitlow v. New York*, the United States Supreme Court determined that freedom is indivisible and that an abridgment of a right anywhere affected the exercise of freedom everywhere. It then undertook to protect certain first amendment rights from both state and federal curtailment. Through a series of subsequent cases all of the first amendment was "incorporated" under federal protection.

The operations of the federal courts were erratic at best in the decade following the first incorporation of the Bill of Rights in the *Gitlow* case. Then, the Court in the case of *Palko v. Conn.*, Mr. Justice Cardozo attempted to create a formula for the incorporation of Bill of Rights liberties. Cardozo, in his majority decision, held that the only rights to be so protected were those whose importance was "fundamental to a concept of ordered liberty" or whose denial would be "shocking to the sense of morality of the civilized world." In effect, the United States Supreme Court, whose constitutional duty it may be to *interpret* and *apply* the Constitution granted unto itself the right to re-make the constitution. The enumeration of basic rights in the Bill of Rights was not satisfactory for the Supreme Court. Rather than carry out the Constitution as it is written, the Court would undertake by a process of "judicial inclusion and exclusion" to determine what parts of the Constitution would be enforced and which would be ignored.

Mr. Cardozo's decision poses many questions for the student of the Constitution. First, one may ask, why is it necessary to set up a new set of

27

criteria when it is obvious that certain rights (those in Amendments I through VIII) are to be equally enforced as they were equally stated in the Bill of Rights? Second, why should the Court not seek either by one generic decision or by a series of cases taken together to state that all of these specific rights are equally ensured? Third, when many rights must be decided on a case to case basis (like establishing what is "pornographic"), why should the Supreme Court burden itself with an unneeded additional set of "criteria?" Fourth, why, when the United States is now and long has been the freest society in the world, should we look elsewhere for standards of freedom? If we were to emulate the majority of mankind we would be virtually slaves. Fifth, by what Constitutional grant of power can the Court choose to ignore a whole portion of the Constitution?

The Court is in effect here stating that sociological findings in regard to standard practices of the "civilized world" are more important than the law is. The Court has systematically refused to directly review the Second Amendment freedoms to determine the meaning and scope of this amendment whether in regard to either "sociological jurisprudence" and its findings or in regard to the legal system.

The Court has had numerous opportunities to review the Second Amendment as various groups have attempted to get a ruling from the Supreme Court on the legitimacy of various state bills which have limited the right to keep and bear arms. These appeals have generally contained both constitutional and legal arguments and the sociological and statistical arguments which have attempted to convince the Court that various laws have been illicit.

It would then seem that a major ruling on the Second Amendment is, to say the very least, long overdue. Precisely what the "Nixon Court" may do in this regard has yet to be determined. In fact, one can only speculate on its willingness to tackle such a controversial issue under the present circumstances. If the new court shows "judicial restraint" it may choose, as have recent courts, to ignore the issue completely, allowing this constitutional right to remain a political issue to be decided in the state and national legislatures rather than in the halls of justice. Conversely, the court headed by the Chief Justice Warren Burger may show judicial prudence and rule directly on the issue constitutionally. The student of this area of constitutional law can only hope that the ruling made, when it does come, will be made by deciding what the Constitution says, rather than sociologically according to what the opponents of private firearms ownership might wish the law to be. Certainly, the issue is far from being resolved as presently interpreted by the federal and state court systems.

# FOOTNOTES

[1]See, *The Military Laws of the United States*, (edited by J.F. Callan; Philadelphia: Childs, 1863), pp. 95-100.

[2]Robert A. Sprecher "The Lost Amendment," *American Bar Association Journal*, Vol. I, nos. 6 and 7.

[3]Joseph Gales, (comp). *The Debates and Proceedings in the Congress of the United States*, (Washington, 1834), I, 435.

[4]*Ibid.*, I, 437.

[5]*Ibid.*, I, 437.

[6]Francis Thorpe, (ed), *American Charters, Constitutions and Organic Laws*, 7 vols., (Washington, 1909).

[7]Henry S. Commager, (ed), *Documents of American History*, (New York; 3rd ed., 1943), I, 89-90.

[8]*Ibid.*, I, 298.

[9]Thorpe, *op. cit.*, VII, 3812.

[10]*Ibid.*, V, 3083.

[11]*Ibid.*, V, 2789.

[12]*Ibid.*, VI, 3741.

[13]*Ibid.*, III, 1891.

[14]*Ibid.*, IV, 2452.

[15]*Ibid.*, III, 1689.

[16]*Laws of the State of Delaware*, 1700-1797, (New Castle, 1797), I, appendix 80.

[17]7 Peters 243.

[18]92 U.S. 542.

[19]116 U.S. 252.

[20]268 U.S. 652.

[21]302 U.S. 319.

[22]283 U.S. 697.

[23]*United States v. Cruikshank*, 92 U.S. 542, (1876).

[24]Enforcement Act of May 30, 1870, 16 Fed. Stat. 140.

[25]*United States v. Cruikshank* loc. cit.

[26]*Presser v. Illinois*, (1886), 116 U.S. 264.

[27]*Presser v. Illinois*, loc. cit.

[28]*Miller v. Texas*, (1894), 153 U.S. 535.

[29]This doctrine was also recognized by the Court in passium in *Robertson v. Baldwin*, (1896), 165 U.S. 275, where the Court said, "the right of the people to keep and bear arms is not infringed by laws prohibiting the carrying of concealed weapons. ...."

29

[30]*Aymette v. State of Tennessee*, 2 Humphreys 154.

[31]*United States v. Miller*, 307 U.S. 174.

[32]*Dugan v. United States*, United States Court of Appeals, Seventh Circuit, 341 F. 2d. 85, (1965); principle upheld U.S. Supreme Court, (1968) in *Haynes v. United States*, October Term, 1967, no. 236. 000 U.S. 000.

[33]A partial list of the cases which upheld this principle are, after the initial 1808 decision of *Barron v. City of Baltimore*, 7 Peters 243, are: *Fox v. Ohio*, 5 Howard 410; *Smith v. Maryland*, 18 Howard 77; *Withers v. Buckley*, 20 Howard 84; *Pervear v. Connecticut*, 5 Wall 475; *Twitchell v. Commonwealth*, 7 Wall 321; and as concerned arms, *U.S. v. Cruikshank*, loc. cit. and *Presser v. Illinois*, loc. cit.

[34]*Gilow v. New York*, 268 U.S. 652.

[35]Cf. Bennett B. Patterson, *The Forgotten Ninth Amendment*, (Indianapolis: Bobbs-Merrill, 1955), espec. ch. 6.

[36]*Ibid.*, cf. cg. 7.

[37]*Near v. Minnesota*, 283 U.S. 697, (1937).

# CHAPTER 3

## FIREARMS AND THE RIGHT OF SELF-DEFENSE

The most important single consideration involving the right to keep and bear arms has historically been the individual's right to defend himself. Self-defense has to do with two arenas of potential coercion: his neighbor and the state. In regard to the state, the individual may find in arms the wherewithal to activate the right to revolt found in many political thinkers. In regard to his neighbor, the citizen reserves to himself the right to protect himself and his property from unwarranted invasion in instances when such guarantees cannot be provided by the state for any one of a variety of reasons.

The early kings of England recognized the right of self-defense. In the laws of Ine (688-694) the monarch proclaimed that "if a man from a distance or a foreigner goes through the wood off the track, and does not shout or blow a horn, he is assumed to be a thief, to be killed or redeemed." The citizen was protected under the law if he chose to enforce the law himself. "He who slays a thief may declare with an oath that he slew him as a guilty man . . . ."[1] In the eleventh century, King Cnut's laws (1020-1023) proclaimed that "if anyone illegally disarms a man, he is to compensate him . . . ."[2] The purpose of the law here was to allow for self-protection. For the next several hundred years, English arms makers turned out a variety of arms designed to arm the traveller while he was on a journey in the English countryside while English law continued to guarantee the individual's right to use them in his own defense.

Firearms in the United States have long been romantically associated with self-defense. The primary purpose of the colonists in bringing firearms to the New World was defense, with the hunting of game being secondary. As the frontiersman moved westward types of rifles were natively developed to deal with the Indian fighting requirements of such men. The "Colt .45" and the "Winchester '73" and other weapons are again closely identified with the life of the rugged pioneer defending his home, family and self against bandit and savage. "Self-defense" is the standard line in many Western movies and television programs. Today, the right of self-defense is more likely to be associated with the storeowner protecting his

31

shop or the citizen protecting his home from the lawless. Of recent vintage is the self-defense contained in the citizen's resistance to riots and civil disruption.

## EVERY MAN A POLICEMAN

In the English common law understanding of self-defense, as preached in the bible of American common law, Blackstone's *Commentaries on the Laws of England*, it was held that all citizens had the obligation to prevent a crime from being committed. Hence, where assault was felonious, a homicide could be justified self-defense even though the question of personal danger was not present. It was legal, and, in fact, required that a citizen take whatever steps were necessary to prevent the successful perpetration of a crime. Should the citizen-policeman be met with resistance, his right to self-defense would be as great as if he himself were a party of the original dispute. The right extended to all forms of resistance to felonies, but not to simple misdemeanors nor to single trespass. No form of fraud was covered by this right. In connection with felonies, it is noteworthy that Blackstone (and English Common law) did not require, or even consider the necessity of, retreat by an intended victim or the citizen-policeman. Life was not regarded as a cheap commodity, and it was only to be taken when other means were not reasonably available to a citizen. The general rule offered was one of "reasonable apprehension of harm." Should such apprehension exist on the part of a citizen he was then permitted to move to take a felon's life.

The English common law extended this right to a third area, that of resistance to riot or similar civil disturbance. When three or more citizens combined to threaten the life or property of a third party, there was the right and duty to resist such a threat, whether or not such a threat was against one's own property or life.[3]

## AN EARLY UNDERSTANDING OF SELF-DEFENSE

In an early state court decision originating in Michigan, a hired man was accused of murder in a homicide arising out of continued harassment of the accused by the decedent. The defendant Pond had warned the decedent to "Leave, or I'll shoot" before he had fired. The case was appealed to the state supreme court when the jury had found the defendant guilty of manslaughter. Three basic questions were asked. First, did the defendant have the right to defend himself, his family, his employees,

32

and his property? Second, does a man have a right to stand his ground or is he compelled to retreat when under attack? Third, may one shoot, presumably even shoot to kill, when under attack?

The court took up the question of self-defense per se as its first consideration. The court held that:

> The rules which make it excusable . . . to destroy [human life] . . . are designed to prevent reckless and wicked men from assailing peaceable members of society, by exposing them to the danger of fatal resistance at the hands of those whom they wantonly attack . . . .

The rules concerning such conduct, the court rules, ". . . should not be allowed to entrap or mislead those whose misfortunes compel a resort to them." Reasonable belief of harm was the only workable solution to the problem of when force could be used during the commission of a felony: where a man charged with [a] crime to be held to a knowledge of all facts as they are, there could be few cases in which the most innocent intention or honest zeal could justify or excuse homicide." The court, the justices held, could protect an individual in cases where, cool reason being impossible, the individual operates under the best knowledge available to him. The defendant cannot be assumed

> . . . in all cases to have great courage or large intellect; and cannot see the true meaning of all that occurs at the time; while he can know nothing whatever concerning what has occurred elsewhere or concerning the designs of his assailants . . . and the law . . . does not hold men responsible for a knowledge of facts unless their ignorance arises from fault or negligence.

The court had no difficulty in underwriting the common law principle which does not compel an individual under unjust attack to retreat. "A man is not, however, obliged to retreat if assaulted in his dwelling [as the defendant was], but may use such means as are absolutely necessary to repel his assailant from his house, or to prevent his forcible entry, even to the taking of life." The court did mitigate this principle. First, only "sufficient" force can be used, not necessarily including homicide. And such a right does not extend to an individual when the altercation results from a non-felonous crime or when it results from an argument in which both parties are adjudged to be equally guilty.

Finally, the court held that a man's obligation to protect his family was deeply rooted in both American and English common law. A man was permitted to defend his property, family, servants, or his master in any instance in which he would be permitted to defend himself. The court held that such a right, indeed, obligation, also extended, as it had in English

33

common law, to the defense of one's fellow citizens and of society.[4] This 1860 court ruling stands as an example and precedent which is often cited in other cases in other states as voicing public law definitions of self-defense.

A second fundamental case was decided in 1909 in the Alabama court system, and arose out of a civil suit against the individuals who had killed a man while the deceased was committing a felony. The court of original jurisdiction held that damages could not be collected by the executor of an estate if such damages could not be collected by the decedent had he only been injured. Alabama law also gave any citizen the rights and powers of a law officer in preventing a crime if such a citizen be the witness to the commission of a felony. The defendants in the civil suit had discovered the decedent and another man, the latter having subsequently surrendered peacefully, attempting to break into a place of business. The felon who had surrendered, Riley by name, testified that he and the decedent, Suell, had been drinking heavily and then attempted to break into the store. They had used an iron bar to try to pry planks off the side of the building. When the defendants arrived, they saw Suell whirl around with an object they assumed to be a firearm. Since the direction of the presumed gun jeopardized both defendants they fired, killing the decedent. In short, the court chose to believe the defendants in regard to their real fear of their lives. The court held this act to be justifiable homicide in self-defense and in line with the state policy of using "necessary and reasonable" force in preventing the commission of a felony. The court clarified certain principles of the *Pond* decision. A man may not only defend his home and property, but he may also repel by force an individual who manifestly intends or endeavors by violence, force or surprise, to commit a known felony, such as murder, arson, rape, burglary or robbery. He is not only not obliged to retreat, but he may pursue his adversary until he is secure from all danger or until he has taken him into custody. If he kills the felon in the process, it would be considered justified.[5]

## CURRENT STATE RECOGNITION OF THE RIGHT OF SELF-DEFENSE

The statute law, or constitutional provision, protecting the citizen when he acts in defense of himself, his family or property, or in protection or defense of his state is guaranteed in virtually every state and in the federal constitution and public laws. Arizona and Washington guarantee the individual's right to use weapons ". . . in defense of himself or the State."

Alabama, Connecticut, Michigan, and Texas protect this right to the person "in defense of himself and the State." Florida, Idaho, Indiana, Kentucky, Oregon, Pennsylvania, South Dakota, Vermont and Wyoming protect the right of all men to bear arms in ". . . defense of themselves and the State." New Mexico, Ohio and Utah reserve this right for "The people . . . for their security and defense." Colorado, Mississippi, Missouri, Montana and Oklahoma reserve to the citizen the right to bear arms ". . . in defense of his home, person and property." Arkansas, Kansas, Maine and Massachusetts give the people the right of "common defense." Alaska, Hawaii, Louisiana, North Carolina and South Carolina basically pattern their constitutional provisions after the federal provision, but have recognized the right of the citizen to self-defense. New York also does this by statute. We shall investigate later how well these noble intentions have been fulfilled.

The right of the individual to protect himself has been under attack. As laws restricting the right of the citizen to exercise his right to keep and bear arms come into existence there are consequent limitations on the individual's right to defend himself. New York was the first to limit this right. In a dissenting opinion in the fundamental case upholding the severe restrictions on the right of the citizen in New York to keep arms found in the Sullivan law, Justice Hill observed that a man of the type of the petitioner, trained in the use of firearms, ". . . who could shoot with accuracy, would be a more useful citizen than one who, if attacked, could only throw a bootjack at his assailant."[6] Since that 1943 opinion was written additional laws have been passed by New York and by other states restricting, by licensing and other devices, the right of the citizen to acquire the wherewithal to resist would-be felons.

## THE FEDERAL COURTS RULE ON SELF-DEFENSE

In a 1960 District of Columbia case the question of pistol and revolver restrictions in relation to self-defense rights was considered. This case is probably typical of the Federal Government's attitude on self-defense using firearms. The defendant Cooke was accused of assault with a dangerous weapon but this charge was dropped under the accepted plea of self-defense. However, the defendant was bound over under court order to answer charges concerning illegal carrying of a concealed weapon. The accused asked the presiding judge to instruct the jury to bring in a directed verdict of not guilty because he had a right to carry this weapon to defend himself from suspected assault. His premonition of assault constituted reasonable fear since he was in fact assaulted. This the judge refused to do. Previously Cooke had been threatened by the assailant and had been

35

refused reasonable police aid even though he had seen the deceased "loitering" in his neighborhood. The defendant argued that his acquittal on the charge of murder had demonstrated the lawfulness and reasonableness of his action. Put another way, the defendant argued that his right of self-defense would be abridged if he were convicted for carrying a weapon for which there had been an already established need.

The trial judge basically agreed with this latter contention by the defendant, but basically stated that his hands were tied by the letter of the law. "There does appear to be an inconsistency between acquitting a man of assault on grounds of self-defense, and convicting him for carrying the instrument used in that defense." However, the court continued, "the statute flatly states that no person shall within the District of Columbia carry . . . except in his dwelling or place of business . . . a pistol, without a license . . . ." The defendant was therefore found guilty.[7] It is interesting that the defendant did not challenge the constitutionality of the law in question.

In an earlier case, dated 1952, the U.S. Appeals Court dealt with an error in a trial of one Wilson. Wilson was in an automobile when assaulted by several men. He used his pistol to defend himself. Like the previous defendant, Wilson was acquitted of the charge resulting from the homicide, but was bound over for legal action because he had been illegally carrying a weapon. The court instructed the trial jury that if it were established that Wilson had had the pistol in his possession at the time of the actual assault he was automatically guilty of violating the same law we saw in the previous case. The appellate court found this to be a reversible error. The appellate court found that an individual was in fact not guilty of violating this law if he had in his possession a weapon at the actual time of his action of self-defense. "The exigencies of the occasion justified Wilson in obtaining a weapon and using it in his self-defense, so that the fact that he had the pistol in his hand as he fired at his pursuers should not have been the basis of an instruction . . . ."[8]

In another District of Columbia decision, the court ruled that the "reasonable" period of time that an individual could carry an arm in violation of the law was one hour. After this length of time an individual would either be forced to obtain a permit or be in violation of the law. This hour's grace period obviously necessitated the presence of the second factor: imminent danger to the bearer of the weapon. Beyond actual repulsion of attack no criteria was offered for "reasonable" transport of an illegal weapon.[9] In effect, if no assault took place, or if the would-be assailant were repelled without witnesses to that fact, the citizen would be in trouble with the law.

## CONTEMPORARY STATE RULINGS ON SELF-DEFENSE

The criteria usually accepted in courts to judge the guilt of a defendant in a homicide resulting from an act of self-defense were well stated by an Illinois court in a 1965 case.

We now turn to the elements which, if present, justify the use of force in the defense of a person. These elements are: (1) that force is threatened against a person; (2) that the person threatened is not the aggressor; (3) that the danger of harm is imminent; (4) that the force threatened in unlawful; (5) that the person threatened must actually believe; (a) that a danger exists, (b) that the use of force is necessary to avert the danger, (c) that the kind and amount of force which he uses is necessary; and (6) that the above beliefs are reasonable. There is a further principle involved when . . . the defendant uses deadly force to those situations in which (a) the threatened force will cause death or great bodily harm or (b) the force threatened is a forcible felony.[10]

The above case is an interesting one in several ways. First, it involves the common law obligation-right concerning care of one's neighbor when he may be under attack. Second, it involves the basic question of retreat in public. Third, it involves the problem of court interpretation of when, in public, an individual may feel his person is threatened and therefore resist up to and including homicide. The circumstances of the case merit investigation.

The defendant in the case was driving on a Chicago, Illinois, street when he saw a group of several youths attacking an elderly man, which man later testified "the only thing I know, he saved my life." He stopped his taxicab and heard cries for help. Several objects were hurled at his cab, breaking a window and severely damaging a door. The defendant testified he fired in the air "to frighten" the youthful assailants. One young man was killed by a stray pistol shot. Since the testimony of the trial pointed to the correctness of his act, little was said of this subject. The court did deal with this, combining its consideration with that of the second point, retreat in a public place. The trial court had held that the defendant could easily have left the scene of the crime, thereby removing himself from potential danger, but leaving the other man at the mercy of the gang. However, State Supreme Court held that "a citizen must feel free to help the victim of an assault" and that "when a defendant is where he has a lawful right to be, he has a right to stand his ground, and if reasonably apprehensive of injury is justified in taking his assailant's life." In fact, the court found, ". . . public policy forbids us to say a person must leave the victim of a brutal beating lie on the street when called upon to render aid." The court took cognizance of the fact that ". . . there have been a number of publicized assaults and homicides, in which the victims called upon their fellow citizens to render aid" without response from these citizens. The court, while recognizing the uncontested testimony that the defendant had not fired at the deceased, underwrote his right to have done so. The trial court had held that since the decedent and his group had retreated, the defendant was in the wrong to fire at all. The State Supreme Court continued, saying that, "they [the original trial court] conclude that defendant should have left the scene of the incident. This allegation does not take into consideration the fact that the gang could have returned and further assaulted the victim . . . ."

In determining if the application of force was correct legally the court found the cardinal rule that cannot be ignored by the courts to be ". . . the principle that [thc] belief is reasonable even if the defendant is mistaken." The use of the pistol was reasonable, if for no reason other than "he had no other weapon." Since the throwing of objects at his cab had caused great harm, the court held that it was apparent that the throwing of bricks at defendant could have caused death or great bodily harm" to him. It is important to note that no definite testimony was introduced to show that any objects had in fact been thrown directly at the defendant, but only at his cab. It apparently was sufficient that he could have been accidentally hit.

The most important aspect of the case, noted as a reversible error by the appellate court, was the principle of law that "the burden of proof never shifts to the defendant no matter what his defense may be, and where he pleads self-defense, it is sufficient to acquit him . . ." of the evidence on self-defense combined with whatever other evidence is presented ". . . creates a reasonable doubt." The court noted "the chilling fact" that men had, at times, been convicted of manslaughter or other crimes when their actions at least bordered on self-defense. The case at hand was held to be marginal, but the court did hold the defendant to be innocent and ordered his release. The tragedy of this case may be found in the fact that he had to be released by an appellate court, for when he attempted to find justice at a lower level of the court system he found such justice wanting. In fact, the appellate court had found nothing applicable which was not already in the law books.

## A LAW OFFICER'S RIGHT OF SELF-DEFENSE

The injury of by-standers in a struggle to uphold the law is indeed a most unfortunate event. A case involving one such unfortunate situation originated in Louisiana where a law officer was attempting to resist an attack by an unruly individual whom he was attempting to place under arrest. The right of the law officer to defend himself against the resistance of an assailant was challenged by the widow of a by-stander who was killed by a wild shot from the officer's revolver as he struggled with his prisoner. The court of original jurisdiction upheld the law officer's action, but the decision was appealed to the Court of Appeals of Louisiana. A state law protected the right of an officer of the law "to use such force as may be necessary to overcome resistance." The officer had already hit the assailant over the head with his blackjack and had failed to stop him; and additionally he had fired a warning shot into the floor to ". . . wake him up or bring him out of whatever he was in . . . ." The courts both accepted the fact that the force used was not undue force. The court found three alternatives which were open to the defendant. "One was to flee, but both his duty as an officer and his right to defend his person negative this choice." Two ideas are noteworthy here. First, the crime at hand was not yet a felony, but only a minor charge of disturbing the peace. Previously it was held by courts almost universally that commission of a felony was necessary to use such force to quiet a person. While the assault was felonious, the retreat at the point of resistance would not have allowed for the commission of a felony. Second, it would seem that the court would have offered equal protection for a private person, not only an officer of the law, since it took note of both the officer's duty to the law *and* his right *as an individual* to stand his ground.

The second alternative open to the defendant was ". . . to engage in mortal combat . . . [but] we do not think he was required to thus expose himself to great bodily harm, particularly when he might be able to avoid this by pulling his gun . . . ." The third alternative, the one chosen, was "to draw his pistol and fire . . . ." The court accepted this alternative as being the only reasonable one and "we think Ogden's actions were clearly lawful." The court found that "the foreseeable risk of harm to others was relatively slight" and defendant Ogden ". . . should not be held to have foreseen . . ." bodily harm to the widow's husband. The appellate court then upheld the trial court's finding.[11]

## UNREASONABLE SELF-DEFENSE

The courts have generally tried to give the right of self-defense only to the innocent victim of assault. One such case illustrates the point. It was decided by the Nebraska court system. The facts of the case were not clear due to a large amount of contradictory and confusing testimony given by the defendant was the aggressor and that the usual defense of self-defense must be considered seriously. The burden of proof to show great need to act in such a way as to cause the death of a man not the agressor was left to the defendant. The act committed by the defendant in pointing a deadly weapon, in this case a loaded .22 calibre rifle, at the decedent in and of itself constituted simple assault. Whether the defendant was justified in killing the deceased was left to the jury to decide. The defendant argued that this was an illegal and unwarranted instruction given by the trial judge because only the defendant could properly judge if he had done so legitimately under due and proper threat. The court disallowed this in saying,

> Defendant here is attempting to avoid the test of the reasonable man. He urges that a person has a right to kill if he has a subjective belief that he is in danger of great bodily injury or death, irrespective of whether a reasonable man would so conclude. This is not the rule . . . . The bare belief of one assaulted that he is about to suffer death or great bodily harm will not of itself justify him in taking the life of his adversary. There must be reasonable ground for such belief at the time of the killing, and the existence of such grounds is a question of fact for the jury.

Since the criteria for judging what is legitimate will vary from juror to juror, it is reasonable to assume that uniform standards cannot be expected even within a given state. In this case, the jury chose to believe that the defendant had not shown probable assault by the decedent and that, the altercation having been begun by the defendant, with retreat presumably having been available to him, as this option was utilized by his friend, the defendant had committed manslaughter, not an act of self-defense. This decision was upheld by the appellate court.[12]

## DEFENSE OF ONE'S HOME

Generally considered an absolutely basic right of free men, the right of self-defense is most often associated with the individual's defense of his own home in 17th century English thought. Jean Bodin on the European continent based his system on the inviolability of the family and of the home. The threshold of one's home marked a line over which no man, or even the state, dared to treat without express permission of the owner. The general principle as understood by the American colonists was that a man's home was his castle. Any violation of this was to be dealt with by stern measures.

This principle was recently underwritten by the Supreme Court of Illinois. In a landmark decision the Illinois court said that in his own habitation a man may use all the force necessary to repel an invasion of his home. Further, a citizen may resist with great force an unlawful entry by one whose presumed purpose is to do grave bodily harm to the citizen and his family. The defendant in such a case, the court ruled, is to be protected by the courts even though the circumstances may not be such as to justify a belief that there was actual peril of great bodily harm. The threshold of the home is to be considered the limits of such a protection, as an individual would be excluded from such a protection in his actions against someone outside his home who was either merely trespassing or approaching the dwelling. Much greater latitude is given to the citizen in his home obviously than is given to him in a public place.[13]

Other courts have been less lenient in dealing with the right of the citizen to deal with intruders into his home. One such case originated in Michigan. The defendant, Hansen, was awakened early in the morning by a man unknown to him who broke into his home and threatened to kidnap him from his home and take him to New York, presumably to set up a photography business there. The decedent, Wozny, was unknown to the defendant, although Wozny claimed to know Hansen's brother-in-law. Several times Wozny bodily prevented Hansen from carrying out certain actions he wished to perform. Wozny forced his way into Hansen's bedroom and attempted to force himself on Hansen's wife. Hansen ran to the telephone and dialed the police number and requested assistance. Several other men were noted in the automobile in which Wozny had been driving. Hansen then obtained a gun and tried to hold Wozny at bay. He had heard screams for help from his wife. When Wozny fled, Hansen fired "at his legs," but the shot killed Wozny. The trial court had found Wozny's death to have been second-degree murder and sentenced Hansen to 14 to 25 years in prison for his actions. The appellate court found reversible errors in the trial court's verdict. First, the appellate court found that in such a case second or first degree murder was never an acceptable charge in such circumstances because this presupposed malice. The court then defined malice.

> Malice requires an intent to cause the very harm that results or some harm of the same general nature, or an act done in wanton or willful disregard of the plain and strong likelihood that some harm will result. It requires also on the negative side the absence of any circumstances of justification, excuse or recognized mitigation . . . . The very facts relied upon by the people to show evidence of malice, premeditation and deliberation clearly would preponderate the other way. The parties had not been previously acquainted. That defendant

41

was scared is undisputed in the record, and his actions bear this out . . . . This, accompanied by the fact a man had forced his way into defendant's home at 1 o'clock in the morning and he was acting under circumstances of excitement, pressure and fear.

The court held that the defendant might logically have assumed that the deceased was returning to his car to summon aid from his companions. "We find, therefore, . . . that there was no evidence from which malice could be inferred . . . [and] that [a] reversible error was committed . . . with reference to both first and second degree murder . . . ." The court of original jurisdiction retried the defendant on a manslaughter charge, and he was placed on probation for two years.[14] The unfortunate parts of this proceeding were that, first, the man was forced to stand trial and that, second, the defendant was still guilty of the reduced charge of manslaughter for defending himself, his family and his home.

Self-defense claims by defendants seem to be much more credible in instances where the assailant is superior in size and strength to the intended victim. While the principle of the *Graham v. Ogden* case above that a victim need not engage himself in mortal combat with an attacker seems to be quite reaonable, still the plea of the undersized man seems to carry great weight in court deliberations. Such a case was decided recently in Maryland. The defendant, Crawford, had been previously robbed by two young and powerful men, Ferrell and Austin. When the two would-be felons attempted to force their way into his apartment, Crawford shot and killed Ferrell. The court noted the physical differences of the two men. "We do not believe that the circumstances in this case show the use of unnecessary force by appellant, a man of 42 years of age with a history of illness and unable to work . . ." when he was being attacked by "a strong 23 year old man, with the cooperation of a youthful partner, when these two had previously had no difficulty in overcoming appellant." The court also found that Crawford had acted correctly when he had obtained the homicide weapon just prior to the attack. "It seems appropriate to note at this point that one not seeking a fight may arm himself in anticipation of a violent attack. Here we think the appellant did have reason to anticipate such an attack."

The Maryland court recognized the right of the individual to defend his home against unwarranted intrusion. In reviewing similar decisions in other states, the court said,

> Most American jurisdictions in which the question has been decided have taken the view that if an assault on a dwelling and an attempted forcible entry are made under circumstances which would create a reasonable apprehension that it is the design of an assailant to commit a felony or to inflict on the inhabitants injury which may

result in loss of life or great bodily harm, and that the danger that the design will be carried into effect is imminent, a lawful occupant of the dwelling may prevent the entry even by the taking of the intruder's life . . . . Authorities elsewhere have recognized, correctly we think, that the rules regarding the defense of one's person and the rules regarding the defense of one's habitation are generally similar . . . . The crimes in prevention of which life may be taken are such and only such as are committed by forcible means, violence, robbery, burglary, rape or arson . . . . The appellant was in his home and as we have already held, was under no duty to retreat therefrom.

In the Maryland decision, in contradistinction to the Illinois decision of *People v. Williams*, the Maryland court held that ". . . the appellant had the burden of proving by a preponderance of the evidence that he acted reasonably in defense of his habitation against forcible entry."[15] On this point it is worthy of note that state law varies considerably as to the burden of proof placed on the defendant. The requirement of the defendant to prove his actions were necessary and proper would seem to contradict the common law tradition, shown above to date back to the 7th century, where the assumption was that a man's defense of his home was licit unless proven to the contrary.

The defense of property and person requires that an individual make certain assumptions concerning the nature and character of the violators. In California, the appeals court held that the property owner may reasonably infer that felons or potential felons are armed and that without evidence to the contrary the individual may operate under the supposition that such felons are prepared to resist his attempt to stop them. The court ruled that ". . . when two people burglariously break into the premises of another, the person in rightful possession is not called upon to give any warning to prevent another felony." It continued that ". . . a reasonable person has a right to assume that the two burglars were armed . . ." and that if warning had been given by the defendant ". . . they would use further force and violence to consummate the theft they had planned or to make good their escape." Since a warning by the property owner would allow the felons to resist more adequately ". . . he would have to pay for his charity with his own life or to his great bodily harm." The court also refused to make the distinction between a wounding and a fatal shot. "If the wound inflicted on the deceased . . . had been slight, could it have been said that more than reasonable force was used?" Had the deceased only been wounded, the court reasoned, the defendant might be rewarded for his poor marksmanship had he intended to kill; and had he only intended to injure, should he be penalized for his poor marksmanship? "We think not." The only question then for the California courts to decide is one of the right to fire at all, and this was granted by the court to any individual whose home happened to be the scene of a felony.[16]

Some states have passed legislation which makes it a crime to point a firearm at another person. Since the taking of another man's life is a serious matter, and one which can be justified in most states only in extremely threatening situations, it would seem that the threat of violence, either in pointing a firearm at a potential felon or in making it public knowledge that one has such a device and intends to use it in case of attack or assault, would be preferable to the use itself. Still, in states which control the use of firearms, even without the discharge of the weapon, the act of pointing can result in prison sentence.

In a Georgia case, the defendant had fear of assault including a threat of a whipping by the complainant, when he committed the act of pointing his gun from the hip at his would-be assailant. The defendant Brocken, a Negro, had owed the sum of $3 to the prosecutor which he had agreed to work out. When he failed to come to work, but was seen in the local store, the prosecutor, Cobb, followed up, and, being unable to find Brocken at the store pursued him to his shack. Cobb was accompanied by four other white men at the time of the incident. Cobb swore out a complaint and in the ensuing trial Brocken was sentenced to six months in the county work camp. On appeal, the state appellate court found that Cobb and his confederates approached "... the house with the manifest intention of doing violence to the occupant...." The fear which caused Brocken to level his gun at the men was that of a "reasonable man." The court refused to decide whether Brocken "... would have been justified had he fired upon the prosecutor." It did hold, however, that "... one who warns another to come no further as he stands upon the porch of his own home with a rifle in his hands ... is not guilty of the offense ...." The court found that the proper application of force as a threat designed to head off potential violence was a most licit act and one which should be defended by the courts at all levels.[17] It is presumed that a well-armed citizenry which stands ready to defend its homes and property is a manifest threat to potential violence by the unlawful elements of society, and is, therefore, a basic right of free men.

In the most recent developments it is not at all unusual to find cases in which citizens have used firearms in defense of their own persons only to be charged with the commission of felonies for defending themselves. In December 1971 an 18-year-old Hollywood, California, girl was bound over by the office of the District Attorney on a general charge of murder for killing a would-be assailant. According to newspaper accounts of the incident, Miss Linda Fitzpatrick shot and killed Larry Herrell, 25, after he assaulted her by holding a knife at her throat while unzipping her dress.

She shot him with a pistol she had in her purse. Herrell was out on bond pending trial on the charges of kidnapping and attempted rape at the time he was shot.[18] A young lady named Suelynn Gustafson who works for "Grogshop" restaurants and had obtained a permit for a pistol because she carried large sums of money had her pistol confiscated along with her luggage because she was carrying a pistol in an airport despite her attempts to show that she had the firearm legally. According to newspaper accounts she has never recovered her gun and her luggage was damaged in the ensuing search.[19]

In perhaps the most perplexing case to come to light, a Yonkers, New York, man was arrested and charged with "reckless endangerment" in a case in which the defendant held a group of juveniles at gun point until police arrived when he discovered them tampering with a milk machine outside his restaurant. While charges were ultimately dismissed by Judge Gilgert Landy, the court warned the defendant that he had "recklessly engaged in conduct which created a grave risk to another person." Police questioned the youths involved and accepted their story that they had been depositing an empty liquor bottle near the milk machine and not attempting to tamper with the machine. The noise caused at 1:45 a.m. had been sufficient to rouse the restaurant owner from his second story apartment.[20]

Conversely, courts have found in favor of some citizens while they attempted to protect home, property or self. In the broadcast ruling, an Iowa court freed a school teacher who had fired his shotgun at a group of vandals who had thrown objects at his home. While it was later determined that these missiles were only fruit, the defendant testified that he truly believed himself in imminent danger. The court believed the defendant in his contention that he had used the shotgun to scare away the attackers and that he had not intended to kill or maim any of them. Justice Fritsch held that, "(the) occupant of the dwelling may, without incurring liability therefore, resort to using firearms to protect his home from what he reasonably believes to be a threat of imminent invasion by intruders." Referring to the fact that there was a group, the justice continued, "it is the law of the land that a householder has no duty to notify a rioting mob in front of his house before shooting into them in order to prevent harm to his property."[21]

Even New York City has allowed defense of property recently beyond what might have been expected from earlier decisions made in that state. Recently, a new hero has emerged for the law and order fans. He is Felix Toro, a young Puerto Rican who worked as a private detective for about five years before opening a small delicatessen in the city. Since Thanksgiving of 1970, Mr. Toro has killed three would-be felons and wounded four more. He keeps a pistol legally on the premises. Of 15 bandits who entered his store, none has left with cash or merchandise. Although he must appear before the District Attorney to explain his actions each time, he insists that his course of action is correct. He was recently quoted by the *Wall Street Journal* as saying, "If they (the police) ever take the gun, I'd have to close the store. They'd take every cent."[2 2]

In September 1967, the New York police were issued new orders on the use of firearms. Essentially, the use of firearms was restricted to three classes of crimes: (1) in defense of self or a third party but then only when in clear and imminent danger; (2) to prevent six specific crimes: forcible rape, forcible sodomy, robbery, kidnapping, burglary under limited circumstances, and, again under limited circumstances, arson; (3) to prevent the escape of a person who is an immediate threat to life.[2 3] These restrictions proved to be unworkable and in early 1968 the New York State Commission on Revision of the Penal Law and Criminal Code recommended legislation broadening the right of both police and citizens to shoot to kill criminals. The primary criteria was to be "reasonable fear" of life or property.[2 4] That is to say, police and citizens alike were authorized to shoot to kill even when human life was not directly jeopardized.[2 5]

Similar actions were taken in Washington, D.C., in 1969 and in Boston in mid-1968. In the Boston case, Suffolk County Sheriff John Sears even briefly disarmed his deputies except in "rare" and unspecified instances. He said he hoped to build "the prototype of a peace-keeing force which relied on anything but weapons."[2 6] Mayor Walter Washington of Washington, D.C., disputed a city council ban on the use of weapons except in grave cases in which human life was endangered. The council had also attempted to remove the "warning shot" from police, and to remove from police the right to shoot at a moving vehicle. Citizens, the police, and even some newspapers failed to see the wisdom of the council's actions and the mayor overruled the body.

## SELF-DEFENSE AND THE ALIEN RESIDENT

The problem of an alien possessing arms is generally quite complex, but one may note that the alien, while he generally is denied the right to hunt, usually is protected by state law as when the right of self-protection is considered. In a Michigan case the court interpreted the state constitution's provision that "Every person has a right to bear arms for defense of himself and the State" as meaning that "The guaranty of the right of every person to bear arms in defense of himself means the right to possess arms . . . and necessarily includes the right to defend therewith, by lawful means, his property." The court reasoned that this was the only meaningful interpretation of the state constitution since an alien cannot ". . . request the burglar to come unarmed because he has been disarmed by the law." The judge also noted that animals often prowl and have to be destroyed. "The right to kill noxious birds and animals in defense of person or property would be but a joke if the means of exercising the right are taken away . . . ."[28]

A Colorado court made a similar finding in a 1936 case. Nakamura, an alien, had been convicted under a state law which proscribed firearm ownership by foreign-born residents. The court declared that it was the state legislature's right to limit hunting of game, but found that the law in question clearly ". . . wholly disarms aliens for all purposes." No law, the court held, can ". . . disarm any class of persons or deprive them of the right guaranteed under . . . the [state] Constitution to bear arms in defense of home, person and property." The court could find in this situation ". . . no distinction between unnaturalized foreign-born residents and citizens." Finally, the court felt that "the guaranty thus extended is meaningless if any person is denied the right to possess arms for such protection."[29]

The protection found by the two aliens above was provided by the state documents, not in any federal document. Whether such protection would be extended to alien-resident of a state without such a provision in the state charter is not clear. In the case of New York, even a citizen is not guaranteed such a right. It is also presumed that federal law to the contrary would negate such state provisions. One may also note in the Colorado decision that the guaranty must be extended to all citizens, excluding no class of residents, presumably therefore including such classes of people as ex-felons and mentally ill, and, possibly, juveniles.

More generally, the right of the individual to be secure in his home and in his person is universally recognized, although many states past and present still violate or refuse to guarantee this right. Without specifying the "how" of the matter, such divergent philosophies as Christianity, Buddhism and Islam recognize this right. Among the five virtues of the Hindu philosophy are "freedom from exploitation," and "freedom from violation or dishonor." The Universal Declaration of Human Rights adopted by the United Nations in 1948 holds several rights in regard to the person to be basic and sacred. Among these are: Article Three which says, "Everyone has the right to life, liberty and security of person," and Article Twelve which requires that "no one shall be subjected to arbitrary interference with his private family, home or correspondence . . . ." Other articles guarantee such items as freedom of taste, religion, property, speech recourse or grievance, and similar basic rights. While the right of self-defense is not specifically stated here, and the material items with which

47

to guarantee these rights and privacy are not listed, it is presumed that underlying these rights is the basic principle of the right of a man, through the use of weapons, to guarantee these rights. This right goes beyond militia training or target practice or hunting; it is indeed basic to the right of the individual to be safe in his home and person. This guarantee would be an integral part of world order.

It is not claimed here that the provisions of the United Nations Charter or of the Universal Declaration of Human Rights is applicable in the United States. Nor is it claimed that a valid case for self-defense could be built on the provisions of these or similar international acts. The courts have upheld the invalidity of this Charter when it clashes with local laws previously when it was found that the Charter was non-applicable in this country. However, this gives a certain if small amount of weight to the basic argument that there is a basic right to be secure in one's home and that he may defend this security.

## CONCLUSIONS

The trend toward more liberal interpretation of the individual's right to be secure in his home is evident, although progressing with different rates of speed in different states. This right has largely been handled by the state court systems. Appeals in this area to the federal courts have largely been concerned with due process of law, except for cases originating in areas of federal jurisdiction, beyond the scope of this presentation. The right has not basically been challenged although the means of effecting this right have not been clearly delineated. This is one area in which the courts may choose to operate on a wider scale. Basically, the wherewithal has been protected only in those areas where the state constitutions protect the right of the citizen to be armed for this reason. Since physical limitations prevent many individuals from being able to defend themselves and their property, it is most logical to assume that if the right of self-defense is to have any meaning it must provide for some device to carry the right into action. While new devices, such as the police-used "liquid mace," do offer some hope, and many traditional instruments have been employed, such as knives and clubs, none of these offer the security, range or handiness offered by a firearm. Until something better is developed, one may conclude that firearms offer one of the more practical solutions to the problem. It might also be added that any transportable device science may provide can also be subjected to the abuses to which firearms have been subjected. Certain new defense devices may not have the permanency attached to them that a lethal shot from a gun may have, but in many instances total disabling of the assailant may be required.

# FOOTNOTES

[1]"Laws of Ine," in Dorothy Whitelock (ed.), *English Historical Documents, c.500-1042* (London: Oxford University Press, 1955), I, 362, laws nos. 20 and 16.

[2]"Laws of Cnut," in *Ibid.*, I, 427, law number 60.

[3]Cf. William Blackstone, *Commentaries on the Law of England in Four Books* (4th ed.; London: William Road, 1811), "Book the First: Rights of Persons," I, 130; also, cf. *Pond v. People*, 8 Mich. 149 (1860), where the court traced the history of this right.

[4]*Pond v. People*, 8 Michigan 149 (1860).

[5]*Suell v. Derricott*, 161 Ala. 259, 49 So. 895 (1909).

[6]*Moore v. Gallup*, 45 N. Y. S. 2d. 63, 267, App. Div. 64, affirmed 59 N.E. 2d. 439, 293 N.Y. 846, 60 N.E. 2d. 847, 54 N.Y. 699(1943).

[7]*Cooke v. United States*, 275 F. 2d. 887 (1960).

[8]*Wilson v. United States*, 91 U.S. App. D. C. 135, 198 F. 2d. 299 (1952).

[9]*Dandridge v. United States*, 105 U.S. App. D. C. 157, 255 F. 2d. 349 (1959).

[10]*People v. Williams* 205 N.E. 2d. 749 (1965).

[11]*Graham v. Ogden*, 157 So. 2d. 365 (1963).

[12]*State v. Archbold*, 178 Neb. 433, 133 N.W. 2d. 601 (1965).

[13]*People v. Givens*, 26 Ill. 2d. 371, 186 N.E. 2d. 225 (1962).

[14]*People v. Hansen*, 368 Mich. 344, 118 N.W. 2d. 422 (1962).

[15]*Crawford v. State*, 190 At. 1. 2d. 538 (1963).

[16]*Mitsu Nakashima v. Takase*, 8 Cal. App. 2d. 35, Pac. 2d. 1020 (1935).

[17]*Brocken v. State*, 76 Ga. 585, 46 S.E. 2d. 738.

[18]Los Angeles *Examiner*, December 18, 1971.

[19]New York *Times*, January 9, 1972.

[20]New York *Times*, November 2, 1967.

[21]New York *Times*, February 20, 1968

[22]*Wall Street Journal*, October 29, 1971.

[23]New York *Times*, September 10, 1967.

[24]New York *Times*, February 9, 1968.

[25]New York *Times*, March 22, 1968.

[26]Washington *Post*, June 6, 1968.

[27]Washington *Post*, January 5, 1969; also Washington *Star*, January 5 and 6, 1969; May 17, 1969.

[28]*People v. Zerillo*, 189 N.W. 927, 219 Mich. 635, A.L.R. 1115 (1922).

[29]*People v. Nakamura*, 99 Col. 262, 62 Pac. 2d. 246 (1936).

# CHAPTER 4

## THE UNORGANIZED MILITIA

We have already taken up the study of the right to keep and bear arms for personal defense, and we have noted the calls for universal disarmament which underlie some of the arguments of the firearms control groups. The general background of a universal defense organization, the unorganized militia, has been set. We have noted the legal existence, under international law, of the *levees en masse*, the body of the citizens fighting to keep their homes safe from foreign invaders. Finally, we have seen how, during the Second World War, the disarmament of England left bare her flank in the moment of need. Against this background, it is possible to reason that a future war might transpire, and that the citizens would need their arms to defend the state again.

The Arthur Little Report to the United States Army proved statistically that the citizen who had firearms training and experience prior to his enlistment was a superior soldier in two ways. First, his training time was significantly reduced. Second, his battle casualty rate was significantly lower than those who had no prior experience. Vietnam should have taught us that the day of the foot soldier is not past, that he will still be called upon to defend his home, his neighbor and oppressed peoples everywhere. His role is still an active and important one.

President Nixon's recent announcements which heralded a generation of peace is a hope we all share. But, many thinking citizens still agree that the best way to avoid a war is to be prepared for war. Should the President's dream fail we must have moral, physical, psychological and spiritual preparation made to commit our nation's resources to its defense, and, if it be the will of the Congress and the President, to also defend in like manner our allies and neighbors. Atheistic communism is just as expansionist as it was in 1917 or 1949. The cries of its leaders bode no good For Western civilization. They will "bury" us if given the opportunity. They will destroy the last bastion of "capitalist imperialism" and replace it with one of the "people's democracies" which have already been responsible for the murder of over 50 million—perhaps even 100 million—people.

51

America has no reason to take a defensive posture on its foreign policy history. It has not sought dominion over the minds and souls of men. Its "colonies" have been either granted or offered independence. It has not been revisionist vis a vis the territory of other states. We need not apologize for our record, for it is as unblemished as any nation in the world. The conclusion to be drawn here is that when America arms, it is for defensive reasons. We have never used our power aggressively against foreign states. Each time we returned from war we disarmed and showed our good will. And after each disarmament we had to rebuild for other nations looked for us to be disarmed before beginning aggression. But in the nuclear age, with lightning fast communication and transportation, we cannot afford that luxury.

The thing which has saved our country in ages past, in all of our many wars, was the "nation of rifleman" mentality. Our men and boys were prepared to leave their homes and jobs, pick up their weapons of war, and go make the world safe for democracy. They simply exchanged their civilian weapons for military ones. But the United States, despite the frequency of weapons ownership, is no longer a nation of shooters and hunters.

Unlike Switzerland, we have no universal military training. It would seem that our nation is moving toward a professional, all volunteer army and away from citizen responsibility. With the abandonment of marksmanship programs by the government we are also destroying any sort of government approved firearms training. The withdrawal of support from these programs is spiteful and meaningless. No one seriously suggests that these programs are training schools for would-be criminals, assassins or insurrectionists. In fact, precisely the opposite is the case. This is not a method of reducing crime or any other illegal activity. It is retribution exacted by certain members of Congress against military preparedness and the opponents of their confiscatory firearms bills. But the danger is that these programs undermine national defense. They create an attitude of resistance in those who had participated in these programs.

## OTHER NATIONS: THE TOTALITARIANS

The Union of Soviet Socialist Republics, Russia, has learned many lessons from those "imperalistic" nations she hopes to destroy. From all of her enemies there are things to be learned which will make her strong. The methodology has been applied in other communist nations as well. One of her most valuable gleanings has been in the area of citizen firearms training. The Soviet Union issues no figures on how much of her budget is spent on

52

civilian marksmanship training, but it is undoubtedly a large sum. The basements of many factories contain shooting ranges and the cost for building and maintaining these ranges would be borne by the factory and not by the Ministry of Defense.

Most astute observers of the recent Olympic Games have noted that the Soviet Union's "non-professional" athletes dominated many areas, but one area in which they have long compiled amazingly large numbers of victories is in the shooting sports. Additionally, the U.S.S.R. always does very well in regional games and in "head on" matches with other nations in the shooting sports. The reason is simple. The Soviet government provides first class equipment and unlimited quantities of ammunition and released time for practice to its heroes. If the threat from the Russians was as simple as the Olympic Game victories, there would be little reason for worry.

But if the typical Russian worker is encouraged in like fashion to learn to shoot, then there is perhaps some cause for worry. And this is precisely the case. Small bore replicas of Soviet army weapons exist in abundance. The Russian weapons are crude compared with our own, but they resemble their military weapons. They function and operate almost identically. Workers shoot with state subsidized ammunition in arms which are small scale military weapons. The cost varies from a small fee to cover a portion of the ammunition to absolutely free.

Private possession of weapons in prohibited in the Soviet Union, save for a few trusted commissars and some licensed hunters in the hinterland of Siberia. But this is a natural occurrence since this is a rigidly totalitarian system under which all human rights are subject to control. The possession of weapons by private citizen could bring about the downfall of the system. One major attempt at assassination of a major Soviet official shows what could happen in that country if all its citizens were armed. However, the Soviet Union does find it expeditious to teach its citizens to use arms.

Shooting clubs exist in other totalitarian countries as well. In Albania, for example, there is a well-prepared People's Militia which is schooled in the use of the Albanian arsenal of small arms. The major East European Soviet satellites have subsidized shooting programs much along the lines employed by the Soviet Union.[1]

Communist China places great emphasis on the people's militia and trains them in the use of the AK-47, the standard Chinese small arm, and even in the use of other larger weapons. The Red Chinese use women in their militias so they are given the same training as the men in small arms. Chinese communes virtually all have firearms training equipment and shooting ranges. Lecture halls are frequently employed to show the correct handling and disassembly of weapons. The militia units regularly undergo field instruction and mock battles.

If one goes through old picture magazines, such as *Life*, he will see that the Japanese regularly schooled their children in the use of firearms. Japan, Italy and Germany produced small scale models of the infantry weapons expressly to teach shooting and drill to children as early as grade school. The communists have followed this pattern, expecially in Communist China. Chinese children are taught a song which tells that "I am a little militia-man preparing to kill the imperialist pigs."[2] During the Stalinist regime thousands of children were trained in this manner. It is not certain whether this practice continues at present.

Cuba, since the communist revolution of Fidel Castro, has again taken great interest in workers' militias and has spent considerable Soviet money on weapons and training for his citizen-soldiers. In fact, Castro's militias are probably better trained than many Latin American national guard units and standing armies. Enrollment in these units is generally universal, and includes both men and women. In fact, it might be fair to call both Communist Cuba and Red China armed military camps in which soldiers and a handful of civilians also perform certain other tasks, such as farming and factory work.

What is indicated here is that in many totalitarian countries virtually every youth, men and women both in some of them, is enrolled in an extensive, state-subsidized shooting and military program. The average citizen in such a country is both a soldier and a civilian. The program, in terms of percentages, far surpasses the American National Guard system. It is hardly comparable, for no universal military training takes place in the United States, and National Guard enrollments are very small in comparison. These nations have come to aspire to the title of "nations of riflemen." To be certain, access to these weapons is very limited and under strict state supervision. But should the need arise these troops are prepared.

No further inferences should be drawn. Crime rates are much lower than in the United States, but Americans would not choose this control in order to reduce the crime rate. The point is solely that these nations are insuring that they have a trained body of men ready to defend their respective systems. The very denial of liberties, such as the right to bear arms, makes these countries authoritarian. But the fact that they are training their population to use firearms ought to be a lesson to us in and of itself. A rough analogy might be that while the U.S.S.R. and other communist nations make material goods for capital investment, a good idea in itself, we would not choose their way of doing it. They are training men in arms, and so should we, but in a different way, a way more in keeping with human dignity and civil liberties.

## THE NON-COMMUNIST NATIONS

Switzerland is the sportsman's utopia as an example of how a militarily prepared population might be created. Young men are required, usually at the age of eighteen, to enlist for six months military service. They are schooled in the use of weapons and are released from service. But they continue to be "on call" for a considerable time after their training. They carry home with them the weapons used in their training so that if the need for their use should arise they will be prepared.

Despite widespread use of firearms and general population ownership of guns, Switzerland has an extremely low crime rate, suicide rate, and stable government. Switzerland has a diverse population of Italians, Germans and other ethnic groups. It has major population centers with relatively high concentrations of population. If widespread availability of firearms were the cause of crime, Switzerland ought to have a high crime rate. This not being the case, one of two things is true. Either Switzerland is an exception to the rule, or the gun is not the cause of crime. Perhaps better law enforcement or court justice enter into the picture, as well as other factors.

Canada, New Zealand, Australia, South Africa and Rhodesia have generally more acceptable firearms laws than major European countries. The need is still present in certain of these countries and several do regulate pistols more stringently than does the United States. Still, the gun has not caused the destruction of these nations.

## THE MILITIA AND INSURRECTION

The United States has recently witnessed several full scale revolutions. The insurrectionists used all sorts of weapons. In New Jersey, the sounds of battle between the police and the insurrectionists recreated a major war scene. In Washington, D.C., the rioters used gasoline and other flammable liquids instead of guns. In Watts, Harlem and other areas all sorts of weapons were found.

The destruction of property was fantastic. This author toured Washington, D.C., after the riot there. He saw buildings which looked as though they had been bombed out after the days of terror. He saw the homes and business places of friends and neighbors reduced to ashes and rubble. He saw armed guards in full battle dress preparing to defend the Capitol and the White House. He saw jeeps with armed troops escorting

55

government employees to and from the places of business in the capital of this nation. And he knew the reason why the riot never spread to the suburbs. There waiting were average citizens who were prepared to shoot to kill.

It is obvious that political decisions were made at the highest level in Washington not to move in force against the rioters and looters. Better suffer the internal insurrection than to take up arms against it, as did the Father of our Country in the Whiskey Rebellion in the state of Pennsylvania. Better to allow this destruction by internal enemies and people made mad by hysteria than to do something to prevent it.

This topic is obviously related to the subject of this book. Do we need not only a major reappraisal of our domestic policies on the right of self-defense, but also on the subject of insurrection and riot? It is the opinion of this writer that part and parcel of the right to bear arms is the right to shoot a rioter, a looter, a rapist or a would-be murderer. And that this right is vested not only in the police, but in the private citizen as well. A portion of the right and obligation shared by American citizens to defend their country is the defense of that nation against internal enemies.

Further, it is this writer's opinion that there is greater justification for shooting and, if necessary, killing, a muggist, a rapist, a rioter, an insurrectionist or a looter than there is in killing an enemy on the battlefield across clearly defined battle lines. The criminal is a brother American with the same opportunities as any other American citizen. He could grow and prosper in this land of plenty if he chose. The enemy soldier is a tool of his ideology and system, probably fighting for a cause he believes to be just, and he is probably there as a draftee. But the criminal is self-serving, he is obviously without principle or ethics. He is committing the crime voluntarily and of his own free will. He is taking a calculated risk that he will not be caught, but if caught he will be turned loose by a softhearted judge and given into the care of a social worker. If he is unlucky he can still beat the system by charging that his Constitutional rights have been violated.

The insurrectionist and the rioter are indicating that because they have a complaint, real or unreal, they have the right to destroy the product of another's labor, even if it be the labor of a lifetime. They are accepting no responsibility for their acts. They are breaking with the system. By their own choice they are as far outside the society as if they were aliens. The looter is the lowest of the group. He is too cowardly to be a front fighter for his "cause" so he drags along behind and, in cool reason, takes another's property. He would be too cowardly to steal if there were grave risk involved. Remove the risk and he is very happy to profit by the circumstances.

From ancient laws of mankind we find that the citizen had not only the right but the obligation to stop or prevent the commission of a crime. The citizen who idly stands by while a woman is gang-raped and the citizen who does nothing while property is burned and looted are kindred spirits. If ever a law of society caused a crime to be committed, however, it is when a citizen takes on that obligation only to find that the courts punish him rather than the criminal.

The state has moved toward expressing more concern for the criminal than for the honest citizen who has attempted to stop the criminal. When, after the Washington riots, Montgomery Coutny, Maryland, citizens began to carry weapons for protection, the county's delegate to the Maryland State Assembly was quoted as saying, "It is common knowledge that many people are arming themselves from what they think is their own protection . . . . It goes without saying that this is a dangerous situation that could lead to disaster . . . ."[3]

In the wake of the riots which hit the United States in 1967-68, many public officials and organizations did call for the formation of volunteer citizen groups to back up police. *The American Rifleman*, house organ of the National Rifle Association, said that "the best police force on earth, alone, cannot stem this kind of mob violence that has swept many American cities."[4] Cook County, Illinois, Sheriff Joseph I. Woods, sought to form a 1,000 member riot control squad, composed of private citizens. These men were to be granted the full power of sheriff's duputies during major emergencies.[5] Arlington County, Virginia, created a volunteer force of citizens under the direction of Police Superintendant James McAuliffe.[6] Montgomery County, Maryland, Chairman William W. Greenhalgh proposed that an initial twenty man force of civilian volunteers be created to help police in cases of riot.[7]

The unfortunate part of this sort of thing is that citizens do technically have, in most areas, and ought to have universally such power. It may serve some purpose, such as for Workman's Compensation benefits, to enroll citizens formally in law enforcement agencies as citizen volunteers. However, the basic right to defend one's country ought to be present without such formal enrollment as an integral part of public policy. Immediate action is necessitated here.

The use of firearms to resist criminal attempts, either by groups or by a single individual, will remain in the foreseeable future. Progress to protect the citizen must be made in two directions: by trained professionals and by citizens. The latter must be accomplished in a manner other than the old style "vigilante" committee techniques. The fight against crime and insurrection is that of the citizen against the lawless. The survival of our way of life is at stake.

# FOOTNOTES

[1] See various recent press releases of the National Shooting Sports Foundation on this subject. Also, see *The Shooting Program in the U.S.S.R.*, (Moscow: Foreign Languages Publishing House, n.d. [1969]) pamphlet.

[2] "Songs of the People's Republic of China" pamphlet contained in the dust jacket of a record of "Revolutionary Songs" sold in Hong Kong. (No date, publisher or other information supplied.)

[3] Washington *Star*, June 4, 1968.

[4] *American Rifleman*, May 1968.

[5] *Gun Week*, March 1, 1968.

[6] Washington *Post*, May 9, 1968.

[7] Washington *Star*, June 4, 1968.

# CHAPTER 5

## WHO MAY BEAR ARMS?

The second amendment indicates that the right of the "people" to keep and bear arms shall not be infringed. However, of the two questions which are presented by the statement, only one can be resolved. The first question, "does this involve all people" can be answered negatively. The second question which is more basic has not been satisfactorily answered to date, "is this a collective or an individual right?" If the right is a collective right, it presumably would have to be reserved somehow to the states and not to individual citizens. The requirements that all males be enrolled in the militia between specified ages would seem to indicate that the right goes beyond the organized National Guard. Opinions of jurists and other learned writers to the contrary, the actual decision will be one of court interpretation for which interpretation the people have waited for some years.

## RESTRICTION ON INDIVIDUALS

The courts have generally ruled that an alien, whether visitor or resident, does not have constitutional protection under the Second Amendment. In a United States Supreme Court decision, validating a series of Pennsylvania court decisions, the right of one Joseph Patsone to keep and bear arms was denied. The case was unusual for, among other reasons, the curious language of the Pennsylvania law which made it unlawful for any foreign-born person to "own or be possessed of a rifle or shotgun." The reason offered was the prohibition of the pursuit of game by such a foreign-born person with such a weapon. Such a person was permitted to defend, by use of such a weapon, his person or property, but the prohibition on the possession or carrying of these weapons was absolute. The plantiff charged that the law prohibited him not only from hunting but also from keeping firearms in order to protect his person and property, which right was recognized by the Pennsylvania law, but which was not provided for on the operative level. "The act in question [also] goes

59

further than the subject of game, and prevents resident aliens as a class from collecting and exhibiting rare specimens of such arms, whether for pleasure or for sale ..." and in this way also deprives such people of on possible source of livelihood. It also deprives them "... of using them for innocent diversion of shooting clay pigeons, or the instructive occupation of marksmanship." The U.S. Supreme Court, however, denied Patsone's petition in saying, "The state not only has the right to prohibit the killing of game, but also the right ..." to prohibit aliens, or other classes, from owning firearms, although such possession is in and of itself harmless. The court's additional remarks again strike an odd note in what overall must be considered a most curious case. "This Pennsylvania statute is preventive as well as remedial. It has one general purpose—to preserve game ...." One method, the Court found, was to forbid killing *in toto*. The other method is "to forbid, in that class of persons who have no respect for the game laws, the possession of the means of killing." The Court again, presumably in speaking of foreigners, recognized the right of the state to "prohibit the owning of a kind of property by a certain class ... which tends and tempts ... violations of the law." The Court also notes another facet of the reasonableness of this prohibition directed to foreigners alone. "As a measure for protecting the food supply of a state, the latter has the full police power to regulate the hunting of its game ...." And it was viewed by the Court that, "In the exercise of this power the state of Pennsylvania has, by the statute in question, determined, upon reasonable grounds and from experience, that the prohibition of the possession of shotguns and rifles is necessary for the adequate protection of said food supply." The Court thereupon upheld the conviction of the plaintiff and the validity and legitimacy of the state law.[1]

The identical situations are to be found in two cases in two other states, where, however, the outcome was reversed, but under protections to be found in state, not the federal, constitution. In Michigan, public law forbade any foreign-born resident to "own or be possessed of a shotgun, or rifle of any make, or a pistol or firearm of any kind." The Michigan Supreme Court, in reversing this conviction, held that this was unconstitutional under the state's constitutional protection that provided, "Every person has a right to bear arms for the defense of himself and the State." The court instructed the legislature that it had no power to "constitute it a crime" for a person to be possessed of a firearm "for the legitimate defense of himself and his property." The Court added, "Game being the property of the state, the legislature may enact laws for its protection, but under the guise of protection of game may not disarm any class ...." The Court gave a number of hypothetical situations, ranging from attacks by animal predators on an alien's livestock to assault on the person and the property of the alien himself, where the individual alien or non-alien could reasonably be expected to exercise his right to bear and keep arms. The Court concluded that "The guaranty of the right to every Person to bear arms in defense of himself means the right to possess arms for legitimate use in defense of himself and necessarily includes the right to defend therewith, by lawful means, his property." Charges against the defendant were dismissed.[2]

The Colorado case involved a situation where the defendant, a resident alien, had illegally hunted and killed 3 pheasants. He paid the fine for the illegal pheasants in his possession, but he appealed his conviction, arising out of the same action, for violating state law contravening the possession of arms by an alien. The Colorado state constitution had basically the same constitutional guaranty found in the Michigan constitution, protecting all persons' basic right to keep and bear arms for defense of selves and property. The state Supreme Court immediately noted that "It is apparent that the statute . . . was designed to prevent the possession of firearms by aliens as much, if not more, than the protection of game within the state." On the operative level, the Court found, "It is equally clear that the act wholly disarms aliens for all purposes." The Court then recognized the right of the state to prevent the hunting and killing of game by aliens. But in drawing up laws in pursuit of this right, the state "cannot disarm any class of persons" or otherwise "deprive them of their right guaranteed under the . . . [state] Constitution, to bear arms in defense of home, person and property." The Court added that this right recognized "no distinction between unnaturalized foreign residents and citizens" and that "The guaranty thus extended is meaningless if any person is denied the right to possess arms for such protection." Insofar as the state law abridged this right of aliens, "it contravenes the constitutional guaranty, and is therefore void."[3]

The question of the right of the state to control the hunting of game on an individual's land in recent interpretations has compounded the problem of limiting the right of persons to bear firearms for the purpose of taking game. In the three previous cases, the state's right to control who hunted game was unquestioned. However, in a 1963 Florida case the state's Supreme Court found that while "The landowner is not the owner of the game, *ferae naturae*, . . . he does own, as private property, the right to pursue game upon his own lands." The Court recognized the state's right to "regulate and protect game, as through the setting of hunting seasons, but it also ruled that the state could not, without just compensations, rule out hunting over a period of years. The Court accused the state's Game Commission of having "confused the ownership of the game in its wild state with ownership of the right to pursue the game." The Court ruled that if this right to hunt game on one's own land were denied "they are deprived of property and about all that is left to them is the privilege of paying taxes thereupon."[4] If this ruling should be taken as a general guideline, it would seem that these property rights would require state recognition of the right to keep and bear arms for the purpose of hunting the game on one's own property. And proper inference might be that one who was an alien, but permitted by state law to own property, could challenge the above decisions, especially the Patsone decision. To do otherwise would seem to indicate classes of property ownership and operation. It is possible that such a decision might operate for the benefit of other classes of persons who are otherwise denied the right to keep and bear arms, but who are permitted to own property.

Such "other classes" of persons may include those who have been convicted of a felony and have subsequently, upon release or pardon, been prohibited from owning or otherwise possessing firearms by local, state or federal public law. In a recent case, a certain Williams was charged under a municipal law of the city of Akron, Ohio, with possession of a firearm. This was in violation of the city's ordinance prohibiting felons, and certain other classes of persons, from possessing any type of firearm. The trial judge took cognizance of the state's constitution which held that all men are, by nature, free and independent" and that among these rights possessed as a result of freedom and independence are "defending life and property . . . and protecting property." The Ohio constitution provided further that "The people have the right to bear arms for their defense and security . . . ." The trial judge then reasoned that after a felon had paid his debt to society he should be restored to full rights and privileges and not be relegated to second-class citizenship. Therefore he held the city ordinance to be an invalid exercise of police power.[5]

Thereupon, the city appealed the case to the Ohio Court of Appeals. This court immediately notes that "Statutes prohibiting persons who have been convicted of felonies, from owning or possessing firearms, have been held valid in states having similar or identical provisions with those pertaining in Ohio . . . ." The Court ruled that the Akron law was legal and a licit application of the city's police power. The court held that such a form of prior restraint, particularly in regard to those who had, in the past, exercised powers beyond those permitted by law, was a form of self-defense which society was free to adopt, "To permit felons, as a class, upon their release from prison, to equip themselves with firearms, thereby enabling them to continue pursuit of antisocial activities, if they saw fit to do so, would present an anomalous situation, to say the least." The Court held that it seemed that the Akron law was related to public safety, was reasonable, and that it did not seem beyond all question to be an unwarranted invasion of an individual right. Therefore the decision of the trial court was reversed and the law upheld.[6]

The courts have generally not been interested in an appeal by a felon to uphold his right to keep and bear arms when such an appeal is based on a distinction between a violent and non-violent felony. Such a case was heard in 1962 in Oklahoma involving a felon whose possession of a pistol was in violation of a state law restricting former felons from possession of concealed or nonconcealable weapons. The plaintiff had previously been convicted of theft. The court refused to make any distinction between this type of felony and any other, be it murder or income-tax evasion. The court held that "By his felonious conduct he classifies himself and places himself in a category different from that composed of the law abiding." The legislature acted properly and licitly, the Court concluded, "When the legislature concludes that a person of that kind cannot be trusted with a concealable weapon . . . ."[7]

In many states it is common practice to restore civil and political rights after the expiration of a convict's sentence. Other states grant such restoration upon parole. Still others grant a renewal of right by direct pardon. What such a restoration means varies nearly as much from state to state as does the time and method used in this restoration.[8] In one such case, a defendant had been convicted of second degree murder in 1939, was sentenced to 15 years in prison, and in 1950 he was granted full restoration of civil rights and political rights by a full pardon. He was found to be in possession in 1956 of a pistol in violation of state law which proscribed the carrying of a pistol by a person who had been previously convicted of a crime of violence. The courts therefore had to determine the status of petitioner's civil and political rights. The court held that full and complete restoration to his former state of rights was impossible. In its opinion, the court declared the the the provisions of state law ". . . prohibiting a person who has been convicted of a crime of violence from owning or possessing a pistol, evinces a clear intention on the part of the legislature to protect the citizens of this State from the actions of that class of persons, who, by their past acts, have shown themselves unsuitable and unfit to own and possess pistols." The court said that while a pardon was possible, the crime committed by the individual ". . . cannot properly be deemed to have been vitiated or destroyed by the pardon granted the appellant in 1950." By the same token, it was held that the interest of society in protecting itself remained the same irrespective of any restoration of his rights by the pardon. The social interest of society, then, in protecting itself from a recurrence of the crime committed by the defendant took precedence in the court's mind over the defendant's rights.[9]

Tramps, beggars and other similar groups of people have been denied the right to keep and bear arms. Because of the lack of ties to community and traditional societal institutions, it has generally been held that these groups constitute a real or potential threat to the community, and therefore the police power of the state takes precedence over the individual rights of the members of such groups. Here, as with felons, the courts have found that individual choice classified these individuals in the nonconventional fringes of society.[10] Presumably, such reasoning allows the court or would in the future all the courts to keep firearms out of the possession of other groups of societal malcontents such as dope addicts, habitual drunkards and subversives.

The courts have found that the collective right to keep and bear arms, whether there is in fact an individual right or not, does not extend to groups, unless specified in public law. Even if granting of this privilege to certain enumerated groups does take place it is a right which is not then extended to unenumerated groups. This is to say that "No independent military company has a constitutional right to parade with arms in cities and towns . . . ."[11]

It is therefore highly probable that an individual will find state protection for his individual right to keep and bear arms if his state constitution provides such protection. If his state constitution has no clause permitting the individual to keep and bear arms, and no clause reserving to the individual his right to protect family, self and property, it is at best questionable and presumptive to assume that he has such a basic right. If the individual is somehow on the fringes of the societal understanding of accepted norms, as, an addict, felon, dissident political supporter, or tramp, his right to keep and bear arms seems at best tenuous. Because a state may provide for its "normal" citizens a right to keep and bear arms in its constitutions, it must be recognized that the courts have, at least in this area of civil rights, given great latitude to the power of the state to protect its citizens by restrictive legislation vis-a-vis firearms and other deadly and dangerous weapons. It seems that the courts have been moving more rapidly in the direction of the alleged protection of society through usurpation of the citizen's rights in regard to firearms. It also seems that in those states with the least urban populations there is a greater understanding of the necessity of men to have immediately available to them various weapons of self-defense and defense of property. In those areas which have greater urban pressures, it seems that the courts have given greater police powers to the state and city and taken away the wherewithal of the average citizen to protect himself. The one area of general agreement seems to be in regard to concealed weapons legislation, with nearly all states assuming the right to severely curtail the bearing of arms in such manner as to prevent other individuals from knowing that one is armed. High crime rate states have generally pushed for some form of weapons registration, whereas other less populous areas with lower crime rates have demanded virtually full-scale registration of firearms.

Until the United States Supreme Court offers opinions in this area it is presumed that the trend toward uneven and non-complementary interpretations by the courts will continue. Hence, no individual can be truly sure of how the court in a given state will precisely, and often even generally, approach an area of firearms/weapons control.

## INDIVIDUAL OR COLLECTIVE RIGHT?

Under the federal constitution as written by the founding fathers in 1787, the state power to create and maintain a series of militia units individually responsible to the state of origin was clearly granted. The United States Constitution Article 1, paragraph 8, clause 16, grants the power to the states for the "organizing, arming and disciplining" of what today are called national guard units. Under the Articles of Confederation, antecedent to the present Constitution as the fundamental law of the land, a similar grant of power is to be found. Article 6, paragraph 4 provided that "every State shall always keep up a well regulated and disciplined militia, sufficiently armed and accoutred." The only new grant of power to the central government under the federal constitution was to provide for employing these state militias in the "service of the United States." In short, the national government was given the power to "nationalize" the national guard units as was done, for example, by President Eisenhower in the integration of the schools in Little Rock, Arkansas.

In the Constitutional Convention there had been bitter controversy over the control of the militia units. Charles Pinckney of South Carolina, for example, had called for complete federal control. Elbridge Gerry of Massachusetts, on the other hand, opposed any federal intervention with the state militias. A compromise was reached which allowed for the divided command with "the Appointment of the Officers, and the Authority of training the Militia (being) according to the discipline prescribed by Congress." Politically, this was a good compromise. Some, like James Madison, recognized that the states would want to use the militias to force compliance with state laws and to insure order. Additionally, some feared the power of a federal standing army, so that it might have complicated ratification of the Constitution if the full control over militias were given to the new central government. Antifederalists did in fact point to even temporary nationalization as one of the grave potential dangers of the new constitution. They foresaw the day when, in order to destroy state governments, the militias would be nationalized and marched away to fight in some distant battle, thereby leaving the home state defenseless against federal tyranny.

As the federalists attempted to answer the arguments of the antifederalists on the point of potential danger to the states should the federal government either usurp the militias to federal use or even disarm them completely, the point of the individual possession of weapons was made. Even if, somehow, the darkest expectations of the antifederalists argued, there was still recourse to the *individual* weapons of the armed citizen. Clearly, *before* any mention was made of an amendment to protect the individual right to bear arms there was the clear understanding of the existence of this right by the very men who had created and now supported the new constitution. There was, as Hamilton argued, no power granted to the new federal government which could be used against these firearms.

To assure limited government, as we have seen, the states, led by Massachusetts, demanded of the federal government, as a condition of ratification, the addition of a Bill of Rights. Lest the concurrent militia power be somehow usurped by the federal government, the individual right to bear arms was proposed as one vital part of the Bill of Rights. Virginia drafted a model Bill of Rights, based in large on its own. Article 17 said: "That a well regulated militia, composed of the body of the people, trained to arms, is the proper, natural and safe defense of a free State, that standing armies, in times of peace, should be avoided as dangerous to liberty and that in all cases the military power should be under strict subordination to, and governed by, the civil power." Additionally, the draft amendment also recommended that "each state shall have the power to provide for organizing, arming, and disciplining its own militia."

The power which endangered individual liberties, it was felt by the Founding Fathers, was potentially federal, not state. Madison's original draft included a provision for the guarantee of all enumerated and implied rights from state, as well as federal, encroachement. In short, these were meant to be rights of the *individual* and not of the states against national abridgment. Had Madison intended otherwise he never would have recommended the adoption of the portion of the Bill of Rights which denied state as well as national regulation or restriction of these rights.

When the Senate rejected Madison's "most important" draft protection, that of state as well as federal guarantees of enumerated rights, it did so for political reasons related to the practical situation not because they viewed the nature of the rights in a different light, i.e., because they saw these rights as being grants of power to the states rather than to individuals. Madison's draft had said absolutely nothing of state militias, as, for example, requested in Virginia's draft proposals. Again, had the Second Amendment been designed to deal with the problems inherent in concurrent control over militias it was have been written more along the lines of the Virginia draft. Instead, this whole area of federal-state dispute was ignored at the time of the drafting of the entire Bill of Rights. Presumably, it was forgotten conveniently lest the clear and precisely worded compromise of the Constitutional Convention be contravened. Madison intended to do only one thing: to ensure the general public continued access to weapons which could be used, first and foremost, for defensive purposes.

A second argument can also be fabricated in similar fashion. While prefacing the Second Amendment with the clause noting the need for, and desirability of, having "a well regulated militia," Madison chose to grant the right to keep and bear arms to the *people*, not to states or to the militias or even to individual militiamen. If one reads any of Madison's formal writings, not only on the drafts of the Bill of Rights, but on the entire area of governmental powers and perrogatives, one notes a penchant for precision in language. So precise is his word usage that there is not an iota of equivocation to be found. In short, Madison's command of the language is such that he could say precisely what he wished to say. Given the background of the arguments in the state legislatures and state ratification conventions, if Madison had intended to clearly state only the right to bear arms of the militia he would have done so without hesitation.

Conversely, Madison clearly states his preference for militias over standing armies, especially and notably in peacetime. Like Thomas Jefferson, Madison preferred these units to the regular professional army, although in time of conflict there was a definite role for the professional army. On the level of theory, both Madison and Jefferson knew that the best defense for the free state was to be found in the citizen soldier who knew what he was fighting for and was therefore prepared to win victory. But to place an unskilled civilian without any military knowledge at all in the field was tantamount to precipitating catastrophe. The answer lay then in preparing the citizen while he was a citizen for potential military service through an active and complete program of civilian marksmanship into the Constitution, Madison undertook to provide for limitations on the standing armies in favor of the concurrently controlled state militias.

Having demonstrated that, constitutionally, the right to bear and keep arms is an individual right from the federal perspective, it now remains to be seen whether the same right is guaranteed at the state level. At first glance it might seem that the rejection of the extension of the rights guaranteed in the Bill of Rights at the federal level to the states by senatorial action might mitigate against their protection at that level. However, this need not be the case if one is willing to work on several hypotheses.

First, the organization of a "well regulated militia" implies an obligation as well as a right. That is to say, that the training of citizens at the state level for participation in any militia activity implies necessarily the access required for practice to these arms. Put another way, because the state militias exist for the maintenance of the security and freedom of the state, this ipso facto confers upon the individual a duty to the state which the state is impotent to abridge. The individual could not otherwise carry out his mandated obligation in the Second Amendment without access to individually owner firearms. In providing for a protection from federal tyranny, the federal government has in effect created a right of man. Looked at from this perspective, the right vis a vis the state is just as great as it would have been had the Senate passed and the states ratified Madison's proposal for extension of the rights to the states.

The second hypothesis is based upon semantics. If we presume that the right guaranteed is *collective* and not individual, how is it to be carried into completion? While the Constitution speaks elsewhere of collectives, such as "the people," no right can be meaningfully applied to a group of any sort unless it can be applied to the individual in some way. Presumably, "the people" means man in the abstract and generally, with exceptions rare. Men generally have $x$ right, although John Doe may have lost that right through some transgression, such as we have seen in the first part of this chapter. It would be totally meaningless to speak of any right of man without being able to generally apply it to this man. The right of the people to vote is a good example of a right frequently spoken of in the general and the abstract. But this right becomes operational when individual men exercise that right. We do of course note many limitations on the right to vote, but that does not invalidate the major point at hand.

The third hypothesis is based upon the Supreme Court's reading of the 14th Amendment in the twentieth century. In effect, as treated more fully elsewhere, the court has come to view the 14th Amendment as if it were Madison's "lost amendment" come to life 80 years later. The reading of the Second Amendment in particular, and the Bill of Rights in general, as a limitation only on federal power fits in well with court interpretations of the Bill of Rights up until the famous *Gitlow* case. As the Supreme Court began its process of "incorporation" of the Bill of Rights under the 14th Amendment and applying the guarantees of rights to the states as well as to the national government, the vision of James Madison became a reality. Even in his own time, Madison had viewed the states as the primary culprits in the abridgment of individual rights. If the 14th Amendment is applied anywhere, it logically must be applied everywhere—even to the unenumerated rights noted in Article IX of the Bill of Rights. While a long time in coming generally, and while not yet formally recognized with regard to the Second Amendment, the Bill of Rights stands as total protection from all levels of governmental tyranny.

The fourth hypothesis here is that the individual and the state can hold rights and powers concurrently, but they cannot share these rights. Sovereignty may lie, at least theoretically, with two or more levels of government (the essence of federalism is dual or divided sovereignty) and ultimately with the individual as well. The individual and the state may be concurrently sovereign, but they cannot share this sovereignty. If the Second Amendment at any point, past, present or future, interposes itself between the federal government on one hand and the state and the individual on the other hand, it presumed by some to be "shared" between the individual and the state. The states concurrently enjoy the right to maintain militias with the federal government, but is this "the right to keep and bear arms" or is it more precisely a phase of a shared power enjoyed concurrently? We here opt for the second interpretation, that this is in fact a concurrent power, not a "right" in the sense of individual "rights." The states have no need to undertake the acquisition of a "right" which they already possess. Rights are something either granted tentatively to governments by the people by contract with government or from "Nature's God" as Jefferson wrote. If rights are granted to government they must have rested somewhere previously. The source most often of rights granted to government is the people. The enumerated "rights" of the Bill of Rights are not contractual grants from government to the people, but rather the simple recognition of rights belonging to the people naturally. The government has accepted a portion of these rights, as it accepted the right to have collective force of armed men in militias and in the standing army. The remainder of the right was kept by the people. Of the right accepted by the government, it was shared by two levels of government. Here we are speaking of two distinct phases of the same right, that of keeping and bearing arms. Or, to return to the original point, the right to bear arms is concurrent between two levels of government and the people. The people and the government do not share a common right; rather they enjoy concurrently two different aspects of the same right. The body of the Constitution properly states what portion of the right it has received by contract. The Second Amendment does two things. First, it recognizes the right of the people to possess firearms. Second, it creates an obligation for the people to use a portion of their natural right to keep and bear arms for the state. Without this statement of obligation the individual would be free to opt to utilize this right or to not practice this right according to his own feelings. Generally, the exercise of a right is optional; however, rationally may generally dictate that he ought to exercise his rights.

OUR VANISHING FREEDOM

Without a Bill of Rights the individual may still legitimately claim his full rights, but not find the wherewithal in the state to enforce his rights. Because the federal government interposes itself between the federal power and individual in order to protect his rights and not between the state power and the individual so as to neglect the enforcement of his rights does not mean that the right exists on the federal level but not on the state level. It simply means that the government has been negligent. One might also rationally point out that it may have been the original design to have the federal government regulate itself through the federal Bill of Rights and to have state governments do the same through the various state Bills of Rights. Failing this the federal government may find it necessary to act. Guarantees of rights, the right to keep and bear arms among them, were frequent in the colonial times. Fearing federal power as the states did they may rightfully have hesitated to permit the federal government to act as their watchdog. In fact, most politicians at the time were far and away more fearful of federal power than of state power. Local abuses were localized; federal abuses would have been universal. In the long run there was much faith in the states to do well by their citizens. Finally, the federal court and justice systems of the time would have been woefully inadequate to undertake the enforcement of federal standards in the states. It was far too early in our history to have forseen the growth of the federal courts and bureaucracy to the point that would have been necessary to adequately handle the enforcement of individual rights in the states.

It is then clear that the right to keep and bear arms is an individual right at both the state and federal levels. There is no such thing as a "collective" right which has no counterpart for individual citizens. To attempt to fabricate such a system is nonsense. If a right exists collectively it exists individually. It may be regulated rationally so as to exclude certain classes of individuals for cause, but it is otherwise universal.

## FOOTNOTES

[1] *Patsone v. Pennsylvania*, 232 U.S. 137.

[2] *People v. Zerillo*, [1922] 189 N.W. 927, 219 Mich. 635.

[3] *People v. Nakamura*, [1936] 99 Col. 262, 62 P. 2d. 246.

[4] *Alford v. Finch*, 155 S. 2d. 790 [June 1963.

[5] *City of Akron v. Williams*, 172 N.E. 2d. 28.

[6] *City of Akron v. Williams*, 177 N.E. 2d. 802; appeal to state's Supreme Court denied 175 N.E. 2d. 174 [1960].

[7] *Renfro v. State*, [May 1962] 372 P. 2d. 45.

[8]Cf. Paul W. Tappan, *Loss and Restoration of Civil Rights of Offenders*, (1952 Yearbook, National Probation and Parole Association).

[9]*Mason v. State*, [1956] 103 So. 2d. 337, affirmed by Alabama State Supreme Court, [1958] 103 So. 2d. 341.

[10]*State v. Hegan*, 63 Ohio 202, 52 LRA 863.

[11]*Commonwealth v. Murphy*, 166 Mass. 171, 44 N.E. 138; see also the U.S. Supreme Court's upholding of an Illinois prohibition of the same type *Presser v. Illinois*, 116 U.S. 252 [1886].

# CHAPTER 6

## THE RIGHT TO CONTROL ARMS: THE COMMERCE POWER

The Federal Government subsequently has reasoned that the Constitution has granted sufficient power to the Congress to regulate the possession and carrying of all forms of firearms. This regulatory power has been tied to the commerce power which reads in part, "The Congress shall have power . . . to regulate Commerce with foreign nations, and among the several States, and with the Indian Tribes."[1] This is one of the enumerated "great" powers of Congress which is implemented by the "implied" power "To make all Laws which shall be necessary and proper for carrying into Execution the foregoing Powers, and all other Powers vested by this Constitution in the Government of the United States, or in any Department or Officer thereof."[2] The United States Supreme Court in an 1819 decision interpreted this clause and stated regarding its effect on the Congressional exercise of the enumerated powers:

> We admit . . . that the powers of the government are limited, and that its limits are not to be transcended. But we think the sound construction of the constitution must allow to the national legislature that discretion, with respect to the means by which the powers it confers are to be carried into execution which will enable that body to perform the high duties assigned to it, in the manner most beneficial to the people. Let the end be legitimate, let it be within the scope of the constitution, and all means which are appropriate, which are plainly adapted to that end, which are not prohibited, but consistent with the letter and spirit of the constitution, are constitutional.[3]

The power of the commerce clause as conferred on the Congress is plenary. Chief Justice Marshall noted this in the classic definition of authority in the case, *Gibbon v. Ogden*, written in 1824. He wrote:

> We are now arrived at the inquiry—what is this power? It is the power to regulate; that is to prescribe the rule by which commerce is to be governed. This power, like all others vested in congress, is complete in itself, may be exercised to its utmost extent, and ac-

complete in itself, may be exercised to its utmost extent, and acknowledges no limitation, other than are prescribed in the constitution.[4]

The Congress has the power to regulate the importation of any item from a foriegn nation, including firearms, and in this respect may proscribe the individual purchase of a foreign made weapon, and it may in fact remove from the domestic markets, by commerce restrictions, any weapon of foreign manufacture. This authority is clear and unchallenged. In a 1915 decision concerning exclusion of opium by regulation the Court said, "it is not to be doubted that from the beginning Congress has exercised a plenary power in respect to the exclusion of merchandise brought from foreign countries . . . . It also has . . . exerted a police power over foreign commerce . . . ."[5] In another decision, the Court held that ". . . a statute which restrains the introduction of a particular goods into the United States . . . does not violate the due process clause of the Constitution."[6] It would then appear that the individual does not have a Constitutional right to keep and bear any weapon of foreign origin, except at the suffrance of the federal government, which policy would be subject to change by a statutory change in public law. This authority has been used most recently in the 1968 Gun Control Act.

The U.S. Supreme Court has, in numerous decisions, since the *McCulloch* case, discussed the power of Congress to legislate in matters involving interstate commerce. It seems apparent from these many decisions that, in exercising its Constitutional power to regulate, Congress may, for the common good, restrict or completely prohibit interstate commerce in specific articles, and may regulate intrastate transactions, as appropriate, to effectively achieve its purpose in regulating interstate commerce. The power of the Congress has been described as plenary and subject to no limitations other than those prescribed by the Constitution itself.[7] For example, the Court has stated, "The motive and purpose of a regulation of interstate commerce are matters for the legislative judgment upon the exercise of which the Constitution places no restriction and over which the courts are given no control."[8] The U.S. Supreme Court has, in the past, recognized the federal regulation of such areas as regulation of intrastate rail rates,[9] regulation of intrastate milk prices,[10] and regulation of intrastate tobacco marketing.[11] It is additionally clear that where, in order to achieve effective regulation of interstate commerce, Congress deems it necessary or appropriate to require uniform licensing, it is within the congressional power to do so.[12] There would seem to be no bar to imposing uniform requirements on persons federally licensed under laws arising from the interstate commerce power, where to except requirements as to intrastate transactions would tend to render ineffective the controls over interstate commerce. This would seem to be clearly within the scope of the Court's holding in *McCulloch v. Maryland*, in its discussion of the latitude even Congress by the "implied power" clause in determining the appropriate means for achieving its purpose in regulating interstate commerce. The permit or licensing system has been generally accepted as one of the most effective means of regulating interstate commerce.[13]

The era of licensing firearms would seem to be just around the corner. On May 17, 1965, the General Counsel of the Treasury Department rendered an advisory opinion concerning Senate Resolution 1592[14] which proposed regulation of firearms by the federal government under the commerce clause. The report offered the opinion that it is conclusive that legislative acts designed to strengthen the Federal Firearms Act, ". . . are constitutional as [being] within the power of Congress to regulate interstate and foreign commerce and are subject to no limitation prescribed in the Constitution."[15] The implications of federal licensing of a right guaranteed by the Bill of Rights, a right not explicitly guaranteed other areas of federal regulation through licensing and interstate commerce control, cannot be precisely determined until such a law is enacted and subsequently subsequently by the Supreme Court.

## THE RIGHT TO CONTROL ARMS: THE POLICE POWER

A second attempt at justification of federal control over firearms is to be found in the principle of assistance to be rendered by the federal government to the states in the exercise of their police power. In the *Kentucky Whip and Collar Co.* case, the Supreme Court held that federal assistance given to the states in enforcing their police power or domestic policies is a valid exercise of Federal power. The Court tied this ultimately to the commerce power, but this assistance can be viewed as a separate power reaching beyond the normal interstate commerce regulation by the Congress. In the above case the Court offered this opinion:

. . . while the power to regulate interstate commerce resides in the Congress, which must determine its own policy, the Congress may shape that policy in the light of the fact that the transportation in interstate commerce, is permitted, would aid in the frustration of valid state laws for the protection and property.[16]

In achieving this avowed purpose, the Congress may impose restrictions or requirements which are applicable in states which have not enacted legislation in the same area or matter.[17] Also, the Court recognized the importance of the federal aid in policing the states in a 1919 case. The Court there said:

That the United States lacks the police power, and that this was reserved to the states by the Tenth Amendment, is true. But it is nonetheless true that when the United States exerts any of the powers conferred on it by the Constitution, no valid object can be based upon the fact that such exercise may be attended by the same incidents which attend the exercise by a state of its police power, or that it may tend to accomplish the same purpose.[18]

If the federal government were then to find that certain firearms ownership activities or expression were legitimately proscribed by the states the federal government, through the Congress, presumably could licitly act to aid states in this area, even if certain states had no corresponding restrictions. In fact, the Supreme Court has said:

Congress, following its own conception of public policy concerning the restrictions which may appropriately be imposed on interstate commerce, is free to exclude from commerce articles who use in the states for which they are destined it may conceive to be injurious to the public health, safety, morals, or welfare, even thoughthat state has not sought to regulate their use.

The Court continued, "It is no objection to the assertion of the power to regulate interstate commerce that its exercise is attended by the same incidents which attend the exercise of the police power of the states .... Such regulation is not a forbidden invasion of state power ...."[19]

## CONSTITUTIONAL LIMITATIONS OF FEDERAL COURTS OF ARMS

There are a number of precedents by which the courts may be guided in any decision involving the right to bear arms which have little direct relation to the second amendment, but which may be invoked as being, in principle, germaine to this right. The right of the public to be protected under state police powers may have to be mitigated in light of Constitutional provisions upholding the individual right to keep and bear arms. The courts have stated that, "The rule of the majority must yield to Constitutional principles until and unless there is an amendment of the Constitution."[20] The courts have also found that "The constitution is concerned with practical substantial rights, not with those that are unclear and gain hold by subtle and involved reasoning."[21] Again, the courts have ruled that "The Constitution is intended to preserve practical and substantial rights, not maintain theories."[22] It is possible that such theories would include the theory that severely restrictive firearms legislation is a deterrent to crime, and that some greater good can be derived from restricting firearms than from allowing the virtually unrestricted use of such weapons.

The court has generally ruled that the language of the Constitution and its admendments can be construed quite broadly. For example, in 1956, the federal courts held that "Constitutional provisions for the security of person and property should be liberally construed."[23] The courts have reminded the government that "The first ten amendments to the federal Constitution are limitations on the power of the federal government, and are not grants of power."[24] The courts have realized that the federal Constitution is a durable document and that "Constitutional language may properly be given a wider interpretation than statutory language...."[25] The court has also ruled that no one part of the Constitution, viz., the commerce clause, should be given precedence over another part. In 1956, a federal court ruled, "As no constitutional guarantee enjoys preference, so none should suffer subordination or deletion."[26]

The courts have historically been interested in the circumstances surrounding the adoption of a constitutional amendment as an aid in correctly interpreting the meaning of that addition to the Constitution. The courts have said that, "Courts do not ordinarily give words used in the Constitution narrower meanings than they had in common parlance when the Constitution was written."[27] The courts have also said that, "The Constitution must be construed in the light of circumstances existing at the time of its adoption."[28] When the precise definition of a word presented a difficulty to the court, it was held that historical research as to its meaning at the time of incorporation into the basic document was licit. "When a work or phrase in a statute or the Constitution is ambiguous, the court must, in construing the meaning of such a word, or phrase, attempt to determine whether an exact meaning was intended and, if so, to ascertain that meaning."[29] Hence, the investigation into the meanings of such terms applicable to the second amendment as "the people," "keep and bear" and "arms" as well as "militia," would seem to be the task necessary for an interpretation of the second amendment.

Another potential solution to the riddle of the interpretation of the second amendment is possible within the framework of early public law application of the right and obligation to bear arms. In a 1958 decision, the federal courts held that, "Early congressional interpretation at a time when some of the Founding Fathers were still living and active is particularly significant, and great weight must be attached thereto."[30] Presumably, the court could investigate such legislative interpretations as the various Militia Acts, the earliest being the Militia Act of 1792.[31] The courts have also given weight to a long history of consistent practice, holding that, "Continuous construction of a Constitutional provision by repeated Acts of Congress and long acquiescence in such an interpretation entitles the question to be considered at rest."[32] Here, again, the courts could imply an historic right to keep and bear at least certain forms of arms from the Militia Acts and from requirements of the U.S. Code that require all males between the ages of eighteen and forty-five to be involved in the militia. Statutory law has long basically required that an individual provide his weapon as a participant in such a militia.[33]

The courts have consistently ruled that a basically unconstitutional act cannot be glossed over by giving it a new name. If, for example, the right to keep and bear arms, as well as an obligation in the same direction, is guaranteed, this right cannot be voided by subterfuge. "The government cannot do indirectly what was Constitutionally impermissible directly."[34] Again the court ruled, "The federal Constitution insofar as it is applicable, cannot be nullified by mere nomenclature in legislation, the evil of the thing itself remaining the same."[35] The courts have also realized that a law may represent a legitimate exercise of power in one respect, but be an illegal exercise of power in another. "A law which is constitutional as applied in one manner may contravene the Constitution as applied in another."[36] Finally, the courts recognize that, "A statute constitutional on its face and valid when enacted, or when given particular application, may be invalid under changed conditions, or when given an application which results in arbitrary and prejudicial discrimination . . . ."[37] Presumably, the courts could view certain state laws which restrict the right of the honest citizen to keep and bear arms while purporting only to control the illegal use of firearms in the light of this criteria.

A most important question with which the courts must eventually deal was raised in a 1940 court case. The federal courts were asked to determine the extent of state police powers. In general, the courts held that, "A state statute, though enacted in pursuance of the police power, is void if in contravention of any express provision of the federal Constitution . . . ."[38] The court should determine if regulation, especially of the type to be found in New York's Sullivan Law, is an excess of police power attempted by a state in violation of a constitutionally guaranteed right.

The court must decide what the constitutional provision of the right to keep and bear arms means on the operative level. The court has set the task for itself to construe the Constitution toward the proper constitutional end that was designed by the framers of that section of the document. In 1941, the Supreme Court ruled that, "When there are several possible meanings of the words of the Constitution that meaning which will defeat rather than effectuate the constitutional purpose cannot be rightly preferred."[39] Just what the proper and constitutional meaning of the wordage and phraseology of the second amendment really mean has not been stated by the Court to date.

## FEDERAL REGULATION OF FIREARMS THROUGH THE INTERSTATE COMMERCE CLAUSE

The passage of the Gun Control Act of 1968 provides an attempt to study the effectiveness and operability of the control of firearms through the interstate commerce clause of the United States Constitution. After much bitter debate, a compromise bill was worked out in the Congress which was weak by the standards of its original sponsors and offensive by sportsmen's standards. However, when challenged in the United States Supreme Court, it proved to be inoperative. One portion of the bill made it a crime for convicted felons to "... receive, possess or transport in interstate commerce ... any firearms." But in a late December 1971 case the court nullified this portion of the bill. In its first two and one-half years, the government had prosecuted about 150 cases.

The case itself is indeed very interesting. Denneth Bass, a former convict, had been contacted by federal narcotics agents who had purchased heroin from him. The agent involved in the purchases had been greeted by Bass at the door at gunpoint before buying seven bags of heroin. Agents secured a warrant and returned the following day to search Bass' apartment. They found a Beretta automatic pistol and a saw-off shotgun, although presumably they failed to locate more dope because no mention of narcotics was made at the trial. He was sented to 15 months in jail, but released by officials after serving 10 months. During the appeal in which Bass was represented by Legal Aid lawyers, Bass disappeared; in fact, his lawyers indicated that Bass did not know his case had come before the Supreme Court.

In its opinion, the United States Supreme Court chided the lawmakers for the "ambiguous" language employed in the act. The court's opinion was written by Justice Thurgood Marshall. Marshall said that the law "was not a model of logic" for it did not forbid the possession of a firearm by a former convict per se; it only forbade the possession of a firearm which could be directly tied to a transaction in interstate commerce. The court was of the opinion that this question was historically tied to state not federal regulation, and that if Congress had meant to intrude in this regulation it was not clearly stated in the law.

However, the court did indicate that a law written so as to prevent the possession of all firearms under any condition by ex-convicts might be

79

upheld if written with logic, clarity and precision. The evils which prompted this law "would be most thoroughly mitigated by forbidding every possession of any firearm by specified classes of especially risky people . . . ." The criteria to determine what people are "risky" was left to the legislative branch. It is probably that the court would eventually have to pass on whether the criteria and defined classes were acceptable under the Fourteenth Amendment. Additionally, it will be a matter of judicial-legislative decision whether a "restoration of rights" grant would exclude the right to bear arms.

It would seem to be clear that the power to regulate interstate commerce is in and of itself not sufficient to allow for federal control in any large degree of ownership of firearms. If, of course, an ex-convict were to receive his firearm in interstate commerce it is clear that if this could be proven in court he would be guilty under the law as presently constituted. However it would seem that most federal prosecutors feel that it is too difficult to tie the possession of firearms by an ex-convict to interstate commerce. It would seem as well that considerable clarification of the intent of Congress and the views of the court will be mandated in the future before this general area of legislation can be considered complete. It is noteworthy that the conservative Justices Blackmun and Burger found that the law as presently constituted "to be clear enough" to apply as valid.[40]

## FOOTNOTES

[1] *U.S. Constitution*, Art. I, sec. 8, Clause 3.

[2] *Ibid.*, Art. I, sec. 8, Clause 18.

[3] *McCulloch v. Maryland*, 4 Wheaton 316 (1819).

[4] *Gibbons v. Ogden*, 9 Wheaton 1, 196 (1824).

[5] *Brolan v. United States*, 236 U.S. 216, 218, 219, (1915); quoting *Buttfield v. Stranahan*, 192 U.S. 470, 492; see also *Yee Hem v. United States*, 268 U.S. 178, 183.

[6] *Buttfield v. Stranahan*, 192 U.S. 470, 493, (1904); see also, *Oceanic Navigation Co. v. Stranahan*, 214 U.S. 320, 335, (1909).

[7] See, for example, *Prudential Insurance Co. v. Benjamin*, 328 U.S. 408, 423, 434, (1946); *Carolene Products Co. v. United States*, 304 U.S. 144, (1938); *Kentucky Whip and Collar Co. v. Illinois Central Railroad Co.*, 299 U.S. 334, (1937).

[8] *United States v. Darby*, 312 U.S. 100, 115, (1941); citing *McCray v. United States*, 195 U.S. 27 and *Sonzinsky v. United States*, 300 U.S. 506, 513.

[9] *Minnesota Rate Cases, Simpson v. Shepard*, 230 U.S. 352, (1913).

[10] *United States v. Wrightwood Dairy Co.*, 315 U.S. 110, (1942).

THE RIGHT TO CONTROL ARMS

[11]*Mulford v. Smith*, 307 U.S. 38, (1938).

[12]*Hanf v. United States*, 235 F. 2d. 710, (1956), cert. denied 352 U.S. 880 and *Arrow Distilleries v. Alexander*, 109 F. 2d. 397, (1940), cert. denied 310 U.S. 646.

[13]*Ibid.*

[14]Introduced by Hon. Sen. Thomas J. Dodd *et. al.*, 19 Cong., 2d. sess.

[15]Memorandum to the Secretary, General Counsel, Treasury Department, from Fred B. Smith, Acting General Counsel, dated May 17, 1965.

[16]*Kentucky Whip and Collar Co. v. Illinois Central Railroad Co.*, 299 U.S. 341, 342, 347, 351, 352, (1937).

[17]*United States v. Darby*, 312 U.S. 100, (1941).

[18]*Hamilton v. Kentucky Distilleries Co.*, 251 U.S. 146, (1919).

[19]*United States v. Darby*, 312 U.S. 100, (1941).

[20]*James v. Duckworth*, 170 F. Supp. 352, affirmed 267 F. ed. 224, certiorari denied 80 S.C. 88, 361 U.S. 835, (1959).

[21]*F.H.A. v. Darlington*, 79 S.C. 141, 358 U.S. 84, rehearing denied 79 S.C. 310, 358 U.S. 937, (1958).

[22]*Faitaute Iron and Steel Co. v. City of Asbury Park*, I.J., 62 S.C. 1129, 316 U.S. 502, (1942).

[23]*U.S. v. Hoffa*, 156 F. Supp. 459, (1958).

[24]*Powe v. U.S.*, 109 F. 2d. 147, certiorari denied, *I.S. v. Powe*, 60 S.C. 777, 309 U.S. 928, (1956).

[25]*Girard Trust Co. v. Vance*, 5 F.R.D. 109, (1946).

[26]*Ullman v. U.S.*, 76 S.C. 497, 350 U.S. 422, rehearing denied 76 S.C. 777, 351 U.S. 928, (1956).

[27]*U.S. v. South-Eastern Underwriters Association*, 64 S.C. 1162, 322 U.S. 533, rehearing denied 65 S.C. 26, 323 U.S. 811, (1944).

[28]*Ken-Rad Tube and Lamp of Owensboro Kentucky v. Badeau*, 55 F. Supp. 193, (1944).

[29]*David v. Schnell*, 81 F. Supp. 872, affirmed S.C. 336 U.S. 933, (1949).

[30]*U.S. ex. rel. Guagliardo v. McElroy*, 158 F. Supp. 171, reversed 259 F. 2d. 927, 104 U.S. App. C. 112, affirmed 80 S.C. 305, 361 U.S. 281, (1958).

[31]Callan, *op. cit.*, pp. 95-100.

[32]*Ibid.*

[33]Fifty-seventh Cong., Session II, chap. 196, Sect. I, 32 Stat. 775.

[34]*Owensboro Wagon Co. v. CIR*, 209 F. 2d. 617, (1944).

[35]*In re Poff*, 135 F. Supp. 224, (1955).

[36]*Lovett v. U.S.*, 66 F. Supp. 142, affirmed 66 S.C. 1073, 328 U.S. 303, (1946).

[37]*U.S. v. Rock Royal*, 26 F. Supp. 534, (1939); see also, *Howard v. Ladner*, 116 F. Supp. 783, where the court held, "the administration and construction of a law may render it unconstitutional" (1949).

81

OUR VANISHING FREEDOM

OUR VANISHING FREEDOM

[38] *Buck v. Swanson*, 33 F. Supp. 377; reversed *Marsh v. Buck*, 61 S.C. 969, 313 U.S. 406, (1940).

[39] *U.S. v. Classic*, 61 S.C. 1031, 313 U.S. 299, rehearing denied 314 U.S. 707, (1941).

[40] *Bass v. United States*, 00 Supreme Court 000, December 1971, also see the report and commentary in the *National Observer*, 1 January 1972.

# CHAPTER 7

## FIREARMS REGISTRATION

Firearms registration, perhaps combined with licensing of guns owners, has been highly touted by its proponents as the major way we have to reduce the crime rate and to solve crimes committed with guns. This writer is deeply indebted to Mr. Alan Krug and the National Shooting Sports Foundation for permission to use their empirical study of this matter.[1] It is this writer's belief that the little use made of existing lists of serial numbers and registration information will shock many. If this is the total use of information, how little use can there be made of information on ammunition and reloading component sales? Probably, we would guess, none. It would seem that the real reasons for registration are the desire to increase the size of bureaucracy or plain ignorance of its value.

We can summarize the reasons usually given for promoting laws creating universal and complete firearms registration as follows:

1. It would enable law enforcement agencies to solve crimes by determining the ownership of firearms through a tracing of firearms serial numbers.
2. It would enable police to arrest persons carrying unregistered firearms.
3. It would make it more difficult for undesirables to obtain weapons.
4. It would reduce the number of firearms owned by individuals and this would result in fewer crimes being committed.
5. It would help prevent suicide.
6. It would help prevent firearm accidents.
7. It would substantially increase the rate of return of stolen firearms to the rightful owners.

This listing is a fair summary of the prevailing pro-registration literature. A more detailed explanation and treatment of each of these points can be found above in this book.

The basic arguments of gun owners, of organizations such as the National Rifle Association or the National Committee for the Right to

Keep and Bear Arms, and of Sportsmens' lobbies can be summarized in similar points. In fact, the major reasoning of this tract can be summarized in this manner. Finally, this listing follows very closely the conclusions of the empirical study of Mr. Krug.

1. Criminals do not register their firearms.
2. Many firearms used by criminals are stolen and tracing them by serial number would only lead to an innocent person, perhaps causing that person to be falsely accused.
3. If a criminal were to be apprehended while committing a crime, possession of an unregistered firearm would only constitute a minor, additional charge which could be placed against him. Where there is no evidence of a crime being committed, police do not have authority to search persons or homes for unregistered firearms without a search warrant.
4. Virtually all of the states already have laws which either require a permit for the carrying of concealable firearms or prohibit it altogether.
5. The presence or absence of registration is not a determining factor in either suicides or accidents.
6. It should be up to the individual to keep a record of the serial numbers of his own firearms in case of theft. There is no need for the government to assume this function for the firearms owner.
7. The high costs of instituting and maintaining a firearms registration program would not be justified in terms of the extremely limited benefits which it could be expected to provide.
8. Registration would be used as a subterfuge to eventually deny firearms ownership to legitimate citizens as is now the case with handguns in New York City.[1]

The crux of the matter would seem to be whether or not the benefits of a registration program, whatever they may be, are worth the costs of administering it. A corollary to this is whether or not monies proposed to be devoted to the administration of a registration program could not be spent in another area of crime prevention with better results. This would have to be determined by a cost-benefit analysis. So far, proponents of firearms registration have not made any thorough examination of cost factors.

Although few people realize it, there is already a considerable amount of de facto firearms registration at the federal, state and local levels of government. A cost-benefit analysis could logically begin with an examination of these existing programs.

Little is known about the dollar costs of these programs, except that they are substantial. But without the availability of more precise cost figures, it is impossible to measure the value of these programs in terms of a cost-benefit ratio.

Some data are available relative to the probable cost of a national firearms registration program. According to H. Richard Cossaboon, President of Management Concepts, Inc., national compulsory gun registration would require "one of the most gigantic computer operations ever undertaken."[2] Cossaboon studied the problem simply as an "academic exercise," since the question of gun registration had often been in the news. Disclaiming any personal interest in firearms registration, he studied it because no one had explained how the government would go about the task if a complete registration bill was enacted by the Congress.

Cossaboon stated that the problem "would require the solving of a least five completely unique systems problems: data collection, data conversion, data storage and retrieval, data dissemination, and data communications, as well as providing a real challenge in overall data systems management." Registration of each gun would require more than 130 characters. He estimated that "it would take at least two years to complete the project and would involve a staff of several hundred people." It would require "a team of qualified experts at least six months just to devise a workable system."

About 5 million new firearms were sold in 1969 in the United States. Several million pre-owned firearms also changed hands. Each time a gun was bought, sold, traded, or an owner moved, the information would have to be changed and updated.

Other costs estimates have appeared from time to time. In testimony before the senate subcommittee to investigate juvenile delinquency in 1968, Internal Revenue Service director Sheldon Cohen stated that the costs of establishing a centralized computer system capable of registering 75 million firearms would amount to more than $25 million, with an annual continuing cost of more than $22 million.[3]

These IRS cost figures were not based upon any detailed cost analysis, but were estimates presented in support of the Johnson administration's proposed firearms legislation. They should be considered conservative. Furthermore, they relate only to the central registration of firearms, and do not include any costs associated with the collection of registration data or the prosecution of violations. They also do not include any costs connected with the licensing of firearms owners which might be included in any firearms registration program enacted by the Congress. If licensing is included, inital costs could elevate to $1 billion or more. According to a study done by Research Associates Inc. for the National Commission on the Causes and Prevention of Violence, "Most registration proposals are either combined with a licensing proposal or vary from the pure form [of registration] by also requiring an investigation."[4]

The highest cost of firearms licensing which has yet been documented is in New York City, where the average cost of processing an application for a pistol permit in 1968 was $72.87. Thus, a theoretical initial cost of licensing and registering the guns of 40 million firearm owners could be placed at $2,914,800,000.[5]

In 1967, New York City enacted a law providing for the licensing of rifle and shotgun owners and the registration of their firearms. The city administration reported that the ultimate cost of the program could be as high as $25 per gun. Using this figure to project the cost of a nationwide program registering 125 million firearms results in an estimate of $3,125,000,000. This cost figure is roughly comparable to the one noted above.[6]

All of these cost figures are in terms of 1968 dollars. They do not include either the cost of enforcing the laws or the indirect costs associated with them. In a cost-benefit analysis, these would be taken into consideration.

Estimates of the number of firearms owners in the United States range from 40-50 million individuals. Estimates of the number of privately owned firearms vary from 100-200 million, depending upon the source. Mr. Alan Krug of the National Shooting Sports Foundation estimates that there are currently "about 125 million" privately owned cartridge firearms in the United States.[7]

None of these cost estimates take into consideration any of the indirect costs to gun owners and the general public which would derive from a national firearms registration program.

Indirect monetary costs to gun owners resulting from firearms registration or licensing programs are indirect only in the sense that they are not part of the direct costs of these programs borne by the government.[8] Examples of such possible costs are licensing fees, notary fees, costs of photographs, costs of fingerprinting, costs of any required safety tests or training courses, transportation expenses, lost time at work, and court costs resulting from gun owners' appeals of decisions made by government officials administering the programs.

Indirect monetary costs to the general public are those resulting from firearms registration programs that in "A Preliminary Cost Analysis of Firearms Control Programs," Research Associates cite as an example of indirect non-monetary costs resulting from a firearms law, the inconvenience to gun owners in New Haven, Connecticut, where applicants for pistol permits are required to fill out a 21-page form stating detailed information about themselves.[9] New Haven continues to require the completion of this form despite an opinion from the Attorney General that such forms are not allowed under existing Connecticut law. The applicant must provide information about his citizenship, medical history, military service, education background, employment record and residential history. He must also provide details on when and where he intends to use his firearms, including the type of firearm, frequency of use, days of the week, and hours of the day.

The evaluation of alternatives via cost-benefit analysis is likely to aid in the determination of just what are the real objectives. Concommitantly, the risk that decisions will be made on primarily a political or emotional basis is considerably reduced.

A national firearms registration program would affect more than 40 million Americans. It would require the commitment of a significant portion of those federal funds which might be made available for law enforcement and correctional activities in any given fiscal year. On this basis alone, a good case could be made for subjecting any proposed registration program to a thorough-going cost-benefit analysis.


## FEDERAL PROGRAMS

There are currently three firearms registration programs at the federal level.

A national registration list of stolen and missing firearms is maintained by the Federal Bureau of Investigation. Data on stolen and missing guns are furnished to the FBI's National Crime Information Center on a voluntary basis by state and local law enforcement agencies. As of March 1, 1969, data on 186-667 firearms were stored in the Center's computers. This program has added to the capabilities of law enforcement agencies. While cost figures for the system are not available, this stolen/missing firearms registration program has received the backing of law enforcement personnel and sportsmen. Since many state and local law enforcement agencies have kept records on stolen guns in the past, the NCIC affords individual agencies access to data acquired by other agencies and eliminates the need for each agency to maintain separate records.

Machine guns, sawed-off rifles, sawed-off shotguns, firearm silencers and other gangster-type weapons, mortars, bazookas, anti-tank guns, and other so-called "destructive devices" are required to be registered under a program administered by the Alcohol, Tobacco and Firearms Division of the Internal Revenue Service, U.S. Department of the Treasury. This compulsory registration program was first established by the National Firearms Act of 1934 and later expanded under the Gun Control Act of 1968. There are now some 125,000 firearms and other weapons registered under this program, which has always been supported by law enforcement, the firearms industry and sportsmen alike. This registration program covers only gangster-type weapons and destructive devices. It does not affect sporting rifles and shotguns or handguns used by hunters and target shooters.

It is not generally known that there has existed, for many years, a compulsory system of registration of firearms which go through firearm dealers. All firearm dealers are licensed by the federal government. Since 1938, they have had to keep complete recordds of all firearm transactions as required by the Secretary of the Treasury under the provision of the Federal Firearms Act of 1938 (U.S. Code, Title 15, Chapter 18) and the Gun Control Act of 1968 (Public Law 90-618, which superseded the Federal Firearms Act on December 16, 1968). These records must include the make, model, type, caliber or guage, and serial number of each and every firearm (rifle, shotgun or pistol, new or used) bought or sold, the date such firearm was bought or sold, the name and address of the person or business from whom the firearm was purchased, or to whom the firearm was sold, as the case may be. Gunsmiths must maintain similar records on all firearms which they take in for repair or alteration. These records must be maintained by the dealer or gunsmith permanently and made available to law enforcement officers upon request.

In addition to these records, each sale of a firearm by a licensed dealer required the completion of a "Form 4473," listing the purchaser's name, address, height, weight, race, date of birth, place of birth and signature. The dealer must record on this form the method by which he identified the purchaser, e.g. driver's license number, selective service registration number, etc.

Dealers are also required to keep records on .22 caliber rim-fire ammunition, handgun ammunition, and components used for reloading handgun ammunition. These records include the date of the sale, the manufacturer of the ammunition or component, the caliber, guage or type of ammunition or component, the quantity purchased, the purchaser's name, address, date of birth and the method by which the purchaser was identified.

Records must be kept by firearm manufacturers and wholesalers as well as by dealers and gunsmiths. Thus, it has been possible for some time to trace a firearm by its serial number from the manufacturer down through the normal channels of trade to the consumer who purchased it.

While these firearm transaction records are kept on the premises of firearm dealers, any information they contain must be made available upon request to the Assistant Regional Commissioner of the Internal Revenue Service, U.S. Department of the Treasury. The Treasury Department cooperates with local law enforcement agencies by making this information available to them as needed.

The records required to be kept by federal law constitute, in effect, a limited compulsory national firearms registration system. At present, the data contained in these records are maintained at the manufacturer, wholesaler and dealer level.

The rigid record keeping by the U.S. Armed Forces on firearms issued to military personnel constitutes another limited firearms registration which is national in scope. While these records remain in the hands of the military authorities, they are made available to law enforcement personnel whenever necessary to assist them in criminal investigations.

This maintenance of records by the armed forces is somewhat analogous to the maintenance of records by an individual firearm owner. Although these records are maintained primarily for purposes of accounting and inventory, they also serve as a safeguard in case of theft. Theft of firearms from military installations has been substantial in the past. Basic data from the U.S. Department of Defense shows that during the period 1954 through 1964, an estimated 16,000 firearms were stolen from U.S. Military active and reserve installations.[10]

While not a federal program, still another type of registration which is more or less national in scope is that involving firearms issued to or owned by law enforcement personnel. Many police departments, sheriff's offices, etc. keep records on the firearms held by their employees. Even though only a portion of all law enforcement agencies maintain such records, the number of firearms so registered is considerable. According to the U.S. Department of Justice, there were 468,000 full time and part time individuals employed by government for police protection as of July, 1963. While not all of these employees have firearms, many have more than one. In addition, many firearms of a specialized nature, e.g., riot guns, are kept by law enforcement agencies and issued to their personnel as needed.

## THE VALUE OF FIREARMS REGISTRATION

Mr. Alan Krug of the National Shooting Sports Foundation recently undertook a study of the value of existing firearms registration programs.

To elicit information on how state law enforcement agencies have been able to utilize the tools of registration which have been available to them, Mr. Krug sent a questionnaire to all fifty states. This questionnaire included an explanation of the survey and requested each agency to report on any cases of criminal homicide, aggravated assault or robbery which are known to have been solved through the tracing of a firearm by serial number during the ten-year period 1959-1968. A remarks section was provided so that each agency could report any additional data which it deemed pertinent to the purposes of the survey. An agency had the opportunity to voice a personal opinion, based upon past experience, as to the effectiveness of firearms registration.

The questionnaire was mailed in September of 1968. After a two-month interval, Mr. Krug sent a follow-up letter to those states which had not yet replied. A final plea for completion of the questionnaire was directed to those still delinquent in March of 1969. The three mailings resulted in replies from all but three of the fifty states. States which did not reply were Alabama, Massachusetts and Rhode Island.

Where cases were reported as solved through the tracing of a firearm by serial number, additional correspondence was undertaken in an attempt to obtain detailed information as to the role played by registration.

Forty-four states reported on the number of murders, aggravated assaults and robberies which they knew to have been solved through the tracing of a firearm by serial number during the period 1959-1968. Three states did not reply to the survey, one failed to complete the questionnaire and one declined to participate. The forty-four states completing the questionnaire reported six homicides and six robberies were solved using existing registration facilities. No aggravated assaults were listed as having been solved through the tracing of a firearm by serial number.

In the two cases in which details of the arrests were given by law enforcement agencies cooperating in the study it quickly becomes obvious that the firearms registration information was not central to the solution of the cases. The details supplied in only two of the twelve cases are given below.

"In the cases cited, two police officers were shot and killed on December 16, 1963, in Honolulu. Investigation revealed that the suspects had burglarized the National Guard Armory and had stolen a number of guns. The suspects had later disassembled three carbines and four pistols and discarded the component parts in a stream.

Many of the parts were later recovered by a search team. Serial numbers of fragmented parts of several guns indicated that the guns had been stolen from the Armory and that the suspects had been involved.

These pieces of evidence were later used in the trial of the perpetrators. Although the identifying markings on the parts were not instrumental in the arrest of the suspects, they played an important role in the successful culmination of the case." New Jersey reported case details on the solution of a homicide:

> One murder investigation in particular was successfully concluded by tracing the serial number of a weapon found near the scene of a crime where the victim was discovered in his automobile,

90

dead from a bullet wound in the head. A disassembled pistol frame was found approximately a month later near the scene. The serial number was traced to an importer in the Washington, D.C. area and led to a dealer in the State of Maryland. The records of the dealer indicated the firearm was sold to a person who used a fictitious name and address. A suspect was apprehended. The dealer who sold the weapon identified the suspect as being the one who purchased the weapon. The suspect had previously used the same fictitious name and when confronted with the information on the purchase, readily admitted the crime.[12]

In addition, Virginia authorities reported that the prosecution of a 1959 kidnap-murder had been aided by firearms registration information, although this information was not used to identify the assailant. The respondent from Michigan noted that, "There is no question that some cases are solved through the identification of a firearm left at the scene of a crime, or perhaps lost in the vicinity. However, I could not provide you with a percentage figure that would be of value."[13]

This response should be tempered by the following observations and notes made by other state respondents.

Oregon: ". . . a number of cases involving serious crimes wherein tracing of a firearm by serial number resulted in identification of the criminal responsible for the offense," but apparently did not feel that the cases were significant enough to warrant manual checking of the files to determine number and details.

Although a vigorous effort was made to obtain complete information on the other cases reported as solved, details were apparently unavailable.

The vast majority of states reported no instances where cases of murder, aggravated assault or robbery had been solved by the tracing of a firearm by serial number. Some were specific in their comments:

Alaska: "Unscientifically, of course, none of our involved personnel can recall any case that was solved through the tracing of a firearm. This recall is limited to our span of experience, which varies from the present back for about 25 years."

Georgia: "This Department has no record of any criminal cases that were solved by means of tracing a firearm by the serial number."

Idaho: "This office has no records whereby the identity of the criminal was made by the tracing of a firearm."

Iowa: "We were unable to recall any instances within the past ten years where cases have been solved by means of tracing a firearm by serial number relative to the categories you have stated."

Kansas: "We have no records of a major crime being solved by tracing of a firearm serial number."

Maryland: "Unfortunately, we do not have such statistical data available; but in our opinion, the number for the last ten years would be negligible, insofar as the Maryland State Police is concerned."

Minnesota: "To my knowledge, no criminal cases have been solved by means of tracing of firearm by serial number in murder and non-negligent manslaughter, aggravated assault or robbery cases in Minnesota."

Missouri: "During the past ten years, no cases have been solved through the tracing of firearms ownership. Normally tracing of ownership proves unsuccessful for one reason or another, but does occasionally corroborate or add to known information."

New Mexico: "We recall no cases solved by tracing a firearm by serial number."

North Carolina: ". . . no one connected with the State Bureau of Investigation at this time can recall any case ever having been solved through the tracing of a serial number of the firearm used in the commission of a crime."

Wyoming: "This bureau was established in 1963, and to our knowledge no criminal cases have been solved by tracing the serial number of a firearm."[14]

Some states reported that serial numbers of firearms aided law enforcement officials in locating stolen guns. These numbers aided law enforcement officers in prosecuting some thieves and in returning some guns to their rightful owners. The comments made on this aspect of registration follow. In most cases this charge was a supplementary one, the primary charge being either for a more serious crime or carrying a concealed firearm without a permit.

Iowa: "We have had some instances where thefts of weapons have been solved by serial number."

Mississippi: "The most success this department has had with serial numbers on weapons has been when a suspect is picked up with firearms on his person. The gun is traced through the manufacturer all the way down the line to the purchases and in many instances, these guns would be stolen from residences or places of business."

New Jersey: "The National Crime Information Center at the State Bureau of Identification makes daily "hits" on positive information regarding stolen firearms and possession of weapons by wanted subjects."

South Dakota: "First, the murders, aggravated assaults, and robberies constitute a very small portion of police business related to firearms. True they get the greater share of publicity, but we and other officers spend much more time on the theft of firearms and the malicious use of them in the destruction of both public and private property."

"The recovery of stolen firearms is a gain to law enforcement as well as to the owner. The owner gets his gun back and we have the opportunity of removing the gun from the hands of a person who may commit one of the crimes you mention. Plus, it can be a great assist in the prosecution of persons who steal and peddle guns in competition to the legitimate dealer.

"Rare is the case when a murderer or robber merely drops his gun at the scene of the crime. Usually, when it is recovered, it is in his possession or under his control, and it always seems to be a gun that he just bought from 'some guy I met in a bar, day before yesterday.' Then starts many hours of attempting to prove or disprove, the person's statement. This usually starts with the firm who manufactured the gun, if said gun has a serial number and is not an import nor a military weapon. Registration would, in my opinion, shorten the route of search. In some cases it has resulted in our being able to trace a theft from an individual and then to the subject."[15]

Some statistical information from the State of New York shows that firearms recovery through registered or reported serial numbers is minimal. In New York state, 741,063 handguns were registered with the state police in 1967. The number of firearms reported lost, stolen or illegally possessed was 18,965. The number reported as recovered was 155. In 1968, 866,623 handguns were registered. The number reported lost, stolen or illegally possessed was 18,672; the number recovered was 384.[16]

Texas reported on the stolen gun aspect from a different angle. Their comment that ". . . upon some occasions we have exonerated some owners who had legitimately sold pistols and had advised us to change ownership in our files" points out another possible benefit of firearms registration. But it also seems to substantiate the existence of an inherent danger—that when a registered gun is lost or stolen and used in a crime, the owner may unjustly be accused. This danger might be expected to increase with the length of time between the loss or theft and its discovery by the owner. It is possible for a firearm to be stolen and the owner not realize it for quite some time. Guns may be stored in the home, often under lock and key, and not be used for long periods of time. If a gun is stolen, perhaps when the owner is away, he may not become aware of the theft until such time as he prepares for his next hunting trip or target shooting match.[17]

The solution to less serious crimes came, according to the survey, in some states. The survey questionnaires and follow-up correspondence did not elicit any detailed information on these other crimes or the role played by firearms registration. Presumably these consist of such offenses as burglary, auto theft, illegal possession of weapons, possession of stolen property, etc. The comments made on this point of solution of less serious crimes are given below.

93

Kansas: "We have used pawn shop sales records to verify that a person bought a gun previous to committing a crime."

New Jersey: "There have been numerous cases in the State of New Jersey that have been solved as a direct result of tracing a firearm . . . .

Presently, daily inquiries as to the ownership of firearms are made to the Firearms Investigation Unit by various police departments. Many times information previously unknown to the inquiring agency is developed through the files and assists them in their investigations."

South Dakota: ". . . the numerous occasions when other crimes are solved directly or indirectly through the tracing of firearms."[18]

## CONCLUSIONS

Sportsmen and gun owners could, if so minded, use Mr. Krug's study to say "I told you so." But that is not the point. The point is that gun registration and/or owner licensing could amount to one of our Nation's great internal legislative blunders. It would be inordinately expensive. When compared with roughly $5-6 billion dollars spent annually on law enforcement, this device would increase costs by 50 percent without materially aiding the fight against crime.

This large sum of money might well be spent on law enforcement, but it would in all probability be better spent on better training, on better laboratory facilities and increased police training and salaries, America could place more men in the field in more and better equipped cars. There are many uses for this sum of money that could better reduce crime.

The Krug study is an empirical one, barely touching on the human side of the question. There are ethical and legal considerations. Legally, there is the barrier placed in the way by the Supreme Court in the *Haynes* Decision. While treated in more detail above, it will be recalled that the Court ruled that registration laws could not be applied to criminals because of the protection granted by the Bill of Rights against self-incrimination. If criminals, those with criminal intent, need not register their guns, this leaves only the law-abiding citizen with honest intentions to be subjected to registration.

Morally, this type of disclosure may violate public ethics. It would certainly be morally wrong to register the honest citizen's guns but not the criminal's. This may also threaten the moral relationship between citizen and the state.

Practically, a citizen might avoid registration by stating he has criminal intentions and hence cannot be compelled to testify against himself. There is little chance that any criminal would register his guns. And, from what we have seen, the use of these records would be of mininal value.

The fact that the citizen must undergo photographing and finger-printing like a common criminal, fill out lengthy and often unnecessary forms, answer many personal questions which are extraneous to the matter at hand, and the like make the prospect all the more odious. When the citizen stops to consider the slight value and high cost of all this, it is nearly unbearable. Further, he recalls that those who would have him do these things by and large do not care to own guns and hence are making more work for those who do, it is even a less desirable prospect.

It is doubtful whether all the guns in America could ever be success-fully registered. The average citizen would most likely bear the brunt in an incident where he suddenly finds that grandpa's old shotgun after the grace period for registration is past. There would undoubtedly be many who would simply resist on principle as well. Registration will not halt thefts of guns from either the government or from private citizens. And it would not halt the illegal manufacture or importation of guns.

## FOOTNOTES

[1] Alan S. Krug, "Firearms Registration: Cost vs. Benefits." (Riverside, Conn.: National Shooting Sports Foundation Monograph, 1969).

[2] H.R. Cossaboon, "Gun Registration Would Create a EDP Monster," *Datamation*, 14 (11):155.

[3] S.S. Cohen, Statement on proposed firearms legislation in Hearings Before the Subcommittee on the Judiciary, United States Senate, Ninetieth Congress, Second Session, on S.3691, S.3604, S.3634 and S.3637. U.S. Government Printing Office, Washington, D.C., 918 pp.

[4] Staples, E.L. and R.T. Clayton, 1968. "A preliminary cost analysis of firearms control programs," [prepared for the National Commission on the Causes and Prevention of Violence]. Research Associates Inc., (D.C.), Silver Spring, Maryland. 63 pp.

[5] *Ibid.*

[6] New York *Daily News*, November 15, 1967.

[7] Krug, *op. cit.*, p. 2.

[8] Staples and Clayton, *op. cit.*

[9] *Ibid.*

[10] U.S. Department of Defense, (Paul H. Riley, Deputy Assistant Secretary). Firearms lost as a result of robberies, burglaries, and other thefts at U.S. military active and reserve installations during the period 1954 through 1964. U.S. Department of Defense, Washington, D.C. August 3, 1965.

[11] Krug, *op. cit.*, 5ff.

[12] *Ibid.*, pp. 7-8.

[13] *Ibid.*

[14]*Ibid.*

[15]*Ibid.*

[16]Personal report by W.P. Brefka, chief, Pistol Permit Section, New York State Police, December 4, 1969.

[17]Krug, *op. cit.*, p. 9.

[18]*Ibid.*

# CHAPTER 8

## WHY GUNS?

Teachers, writers, news commentators and others have attempted to answer this question: why do guns intrigue us so much? Perhaps a more objective way to state the question would be: Why have firearms so polarized us? It would seem that one cannot be neutral on the question of the rights of the private citizen to keep and bear arms. He must either be for or against the issue totally. Is there some psychological attraction or repulsion of these objects which escapes notice by the scientist? Or is it that they are symbols of something which some men would call good and others evil?

## 1. WHO ARE THE OPPONENTS OF FIREARMS?

While civil libertarians and/or liberals have sought in recent years to expand the meaning of virtually every portion, phrase and clause of the Constitution of the United States, the one area not so touched has been the Second Amendment to that Constitution. The American Civil Liberties Union, which has long championed "civil rights" causes has publicly announced its intention to support an anti-firearms public policy. Usually associated with movement left of center politically, the ACLU seems typical of a liberal reluctance to support the verbiage of the second item in the Bill of Rights as it might pertain to the private citizen. Paradoxically conservative spokesmen have also condemned the broad interpretation of the same portion of the Constitution. The extremes of right and left on the political spectrum, the para-military and extremist groups of the right and the militant groups of the left have at least one case in common: the right to keep and bear arms. But it's far too simplistic to say the "middle America" does not support the right and "extremist America" does find meaning in the individual right to keep and bear arms. The large city press, led by the Washington *Post* and the New York *Times*, is certainly a strong supporter of restrictive firearms policy, and hence this cause is vocalized.

A wide variety of "non-political" groups have appeared in the press over the past few years asking for "responsible" firearms controls. The

OUR VANISHING FREEDOM

World Council of Churches, and a number of its independent members and
associate groups, have backed their demands for firearms controls by letter
writing campaigns and petitions. The power of the sermon in church gives
the opinion of the clergy great weight with members. One might contrast
this position with that of the early colonial clergy, notably in New
England, who led their male parishoners in martial drill after services. The
ACLU, supposedly a defender of constitutional rights, has called upon its
member and associate groups to "help mobilize public support for the
strongest possible legislation to control gun sales and to require gun owners
to register their weapons." According to the American Civil Liberties
Union, and its board of directors, such legislation is "constitutionally
essential" in our society. The individual possession of weapons was referred
to as "stockpiling," presumably a negative value-laden term, is "creating an
atmosphere stifling to the enjoyment of civil liberties" as these liberties are
interpreted by the ACLU. To conclude, the ACLU suggested that "unless
strong gun control regulation legislation is adopted, the freedoms associated
with civilized society cannot be fully enjoyed."[1]

The Americans for Democratic Action (ADA) has also joined in the
fight against firearms. In the summer of 1969, the ADA suggested that a
good way to fight crime would be to confiscate all publicly owned
handguns and then store all long arms (rifles and shotguns) in public
warehouses where access would be stringently regulated. The liberal group
rejected an alternate proposal which would "merely" recommend total
registration. The delegates to the ADA's 22nd annual convention in Washington, D.C., held that America "should be totally disarmed."[2]

A wide array of Hollywood and Broadway movie stars and starlets
have expressed their negative sentiments in regard to the right to keep and
bear arms. Eydie Gorme, a popular singer, has said that she cannot
understand why anyone would object to registration because, "we're only
asking that they be registered like cars, or fishermen, or drivers (sic)." One
of the pressures brought on Congress in 1968 to force stiffer gun control
laws was that of a group of Broadway stars who staged a show, the
purpose of which was to ask for support for bills then under Congressional
consideration. Among those participating were: Betsy Palmer, Robert
Goulet, Joel Grey, William Redfield and Eydie Gorme. Late night television
fans know of the efforts of some of the personalities to force gun control
on their viewers.

Mental Health Associations have engaged in politics often to support
additional anti-guns programs. Commercial businesses, including Montgomery Ward's, have urged gun control through newspapers advertisements.
A full page ad favoring strong gun control can be found frequently in the
New York *Times* and the Washington *Post*. Obviously, the anti-firearms
groups have a great amount of money available to them.

98

Even state and local governmental organizations have become involved in recommending such legislation restricting firearms ownership. The federal government has been active in filibustering for legislation through the Internal Revenue Service which has sought additional power through the control and administration of new federal legislation. Recently, the head of IRS ran afoul of Congress for using his position to call for political action in this area. The Metropolitan Washington Council of Governments (COG) has been particularly active in this area as well.[3]

The best known liberal columnists have taken, if they will excuse the pun, pot shots at the right to bear arms. Morrie Ryskind, writing in the Washington *Star*, admitted that after his first column against firearms he received 166 pieces of mail against his position and 2 supporting him. Still, he implies that the gun-owning fraternity are "adherents of civil disobedience" for holding to the position that the Constitution protects the individual in his right to bear and keep arms.[4] Art Buchwald, widely syndicated, wrote that "The United States is a very special type of insane asylum in that all the inmates are permitted to have guns." Scoffing at the constitutional provision, Buchwald continued, "These guns are sold right in the hospital ... because when the hospital was built in 1775 the Founders wrote it into the rules."[5]

## 2. PROFESSOR HOFSTADTER AND THE RIGHT TO BEAR ARMS

That Richard Hofstadter is an eminently qualified American historian, whose credentials are well-nigh impeccable, is firmly established; his many books are being read today across the United States and in most foreign countries. There is probably not a major college library which lacks all of his books. His name would be in any social scientist's list of "Ten best known and respected historians." But everyone has at least one weakness, one bad publication, one pet peeve which prompts him to write where he should not, one publication which, years later in retrospect, he determines would have better gone unpublished. Conversely, there are journals who want so badly to have a "Big Name" that they will publish anything that Mr. Great will put his name to, no questions asked. Here we find such a wedding of mistakes and grasping.

An overview would be that Mr. Hofstadter has produced an invective against firearms ownership in an attack so laden with misinformation, innuendo and illogical conclusion that, if he were writing for the *American Historical Review* or delivering it as a paper to the American Historical Association, his conclusions would be immediately attacked by even the newest member or subscriber. Writing as he was for the newly politicized *American Heritage* magazine, Professor Hofstadter could give full vent to his own feelings and prejudices without fear of criticism. It is perhaps good for the soul to confess at times one's irrational feelings. Too much objectivity breeds repression of sentiment and of one's humanity. However, to offer one's name to a noble cause, especially when that name has been tantamount to the epitome of logic, fashioned reason and objectivity—that is another matter. Had the article been clearly labeled what it was, a guest shot at Hofstadter's least favorite institution and right, it would have been far more acceptable.

His basic theses are: (1) that Americans find guns "enthralling" and project these into phallic symbols of "manhood rituals;" (2) the right to bear arms is derived almost exclusively from the founding fathers fear of standing armies; (3) that since America is the only modern nation which still clings to the right to keep and bear arms, we must be wrong and they right; (4) that television, movies and so on continue to encourage violence via the semi-hero of the script, the man with the gun—be he Matt Dillon, Al Capone, Jesse James, Billy the Kid or Bonnie and Clyde—and that this style of programming is in response to America as a gun culture. Remove this dedication to guns, we remove violence from our entertainment. All these attacks are old-hat and all can be answered head-on.

## MR. BAKAL AND THE RIGHT TO BEAR ARMS

Carl Bakal is probably the best known of the anti-guns advocates, at least of those whose careers have been largely devoted to anti-guns polemics, as opposed to those who have jumped on a politically expedient bandwagon, like Hofstadter, John Glenn, or Senator Ted Kennedy. His book against firearms, *The Right to Bear Arms*, has appeared in both hardcover and now in slightly revised form in paperback. It is really a mass of misinformation, innuendo and, even, at times, near plagerism (his chapter on the constitutional aspects of this right is nearly a verbatim copy of an old article from a law review, originally published around the turn of the century). Selections were even reprinted in the normally rational *Readers Digest*. Certainly, he has influenced many even though this writer would not consider his book to be the best, most rational or most logical statement on his side of the issue. He has confused fact with opinion, especially in his unwarranted and unjustified attacks on the National Rifle Association. In the parts of his works dealing the the N.R.A. and gun magazines, he demonstrates the power and glory of yellow journalism at its strongest.

His use and perhaps misuse of statistical information lead the unknowing reader down the garden path to but one possible conclusion: that guns ought to be banned outright, and, along with this, most gun owners might be best locked away in mental hospitals for their own, as well as society's, protection. This picture fits in very well with the Herblock cartoons of the lunatic gun owner with bandoleers, machine guns and a starry-eyed gaze. Bakal attempts to tie, by innuendo, the rise of crime to the fact that America is, in his words, "an armed camp." The citizen is to be frightened by the fact that, on the average, one home out of two contains one or more guns. And the firearms fraternity is to be frightened into giving up its guns because other nations have lower crime rates. He feels that it is logical to reason that because gun dealers are licensed, so should owners. Precisely how this last point is a bit logical escapes the present writer. One might assume that because dealers in golf balls are somehow licensed, so should golf ball owners.

Because "most civilized" nations license firearms, Bakal believes so should the United States. This ignores the fact that the United States has been a leader in the advocacy of freedom, and, by the same logic, because other nations license news reporters or control the press more stringently, so should the United States. Bakal seems to favor outright confiscation of all privately owned firearms, given his choice. The assassinations of Dr. King, Senator Kennedy and President Kennedy are foremost among Bakal's examples of crimes which probably could have been prevented had the nation decided to adopt his "rational" plan for gun control. This is an easy thing to say but an impossible one to prove. There is absolutely no proof available which would indicate that any individual bent on a crime would be prevented from committing that crime by registration, confiscation or other firearms control legislation.

The American sportsmen, in Bakal's future utopia, should be satisfied with "shotguns and air gun," and these presumably to be used for sporting purposes only at authorized (and undoubtedly licensed) shooting clubs or on authorized hunting ranges and preserves. The right of access to weapons for self-defense seems to be out of his schema completely, as does the right to hunt larger species of game with a rifle or handgun. The fact that shotguns can be illegally altered to become deadly weapons to be used by those bent on crime apparently does not fit in well with Bakal's plan so this aspect of potential criminal activity is ignored.

Presumably, disarmament would accelerate and armed guards and perhaps armed police or internal military forces would be phased out. He believes that this disarmament of citizens has been culminated in England, and citizens and police are safer. This begs the question of the armed camp which the British have faced in Northern Ireland. And it ignores the potential of "zip guns," other homemade devices and explosives, such as "molotov cocktails" which are the stock in trade of insurrectionists.

Bakal's inferences concerning almost totally disarmed Japan are equally invalid because of the Japanese penchant for knives as substitute for firearms. The high Japanese assassination record, the unusually high destructive bent of Japanese rioters in recent socialist and student strikes, and the strict law enforcement in Japan are factors which must be considered before comparing Japan with the United States. The recent Japanese socialist-inspired riots against the U.S.-Japan Security Treaty, for return of Okinawa and against policies of the Sato government have shown that insurrectionist Japanese do not seem to need firearms, or, at least that they can find worthy substitutes if necessary.

Other nations compared with the United States include Sweden, the great socialist-bureaucratic state which places welfarism over individuality and liberty; France, where, like Japan, rioters have not been handicapped by the lack of available firearms; and the Netherlands, where a high population density precludes great use of firearms. It is not meant that these examples can be easily or completely dismissed in a sentence; rather, that, generally, these are not examples to emulate in all things. The argument that "all the other nations are doing it" is hardly a valid one. This sort of situation ethics and peer group value structuring is not the best approach. If the basic values of a country are sound, it need not look for outside examples on which to base its laws.

Mr. Bakal states his argument in passionate, emotional and even logical fashion at times. The attention paid to his crusade may have been one of the multiple causes of the recent laws and other proposed legislation. His work is worthy of study, for it contains the bulk of the argments against the retention of the Second Amendment. It is possible, however, to answer his arguments point by point.

## 4. THUNDER ON THE RIGHT

While it comes as no surprise to anyone that the major opposition to firearms comes from the "liberal bloc" in American politics, it does come at least as a bit of a surprise that some writers of the political right have been given of late to taking the side of firearms control. This position is surprising for it seems a bit hypocritical for several reasons. First, most conservatives have adopted at least some degree of the libertarianism of the 19th century liberal writers, notably of John Stuart Mill. Second, the mechanisms of gun control invariably involve more and larger government, something that is usually quite abhorrent to the conservative. Third, there the

 the

 the

 the

is the basic conservative commitment to property rights, of which guns are one form. Fourth, there is the paternalistic "big brother" mentality of guns registration and licensing. The assumption is that the individual needs government to help him control his property. This argument is never stated, for example, about the need for governmental control over houses through Urban Renewal and so on.

Jenkin Lloyd Jones, for example, feels that "it would seem "reasonable" that no American "be permitted to possess a gun without placing the gun's serial number and the identity and fingerprints" of the owner in the hands of the police. Further, the police should, in his view, obtain a sample slug from each weapon to keep on file for possible match-up with a bullet found on the scene of a crime. This is not a "total answer" but it will do in Jones' view until something better and more effective comes along. While he favors heavy criminal penalties for illegal use or illegal possession of a gun, Jones creates no practical safeguard for the average citizen. He correctly reasons that incidences of firearms ownership and use increase with the breakdown of law and order.

James Jackson Kilpatrick is even stronger in his stand against firearms. Believing that the "tools of violence" must be subjected to "sensible control" Kilpatrick urged passage of highly restrictive legislation in mid-1968. Beginning his attack on firearms in a manner reminiscent of Carl Bakal's emotionalism, he denies that the Second Amendment can stand on its own, but believes it to be vitally interconnected with the militia. He cannot understand why sportsmen's groups in general and the National Rifle Association in particular have opposed additional federal legislation in the matter of gun control.

Having dismissed a portion of the opposition as being essentially ill-informed or misinformed about Congressional intent, which he believes to be quite innocent and worthy, he concludes that many opponents of gun laws are "full of a kooky paranoia." He feels that there is nothing to be feared from the communists by way of an invasion or take-over in this country. The constitutional argument for a right to bear arms he calls "groundless." Proposed federal legislation which he supported—in essence, the 1968 gun control act—he felt would not have "the slightest effect" on hunters or legitimate sportsment or shooters.

The title of his article "It's High Time for Federal Gun-Control Law" tells it exactly like it is in his column. He feels that the type of law which he would support would not interfere with antique arms collectors despite the fact that there are many arms of collectors' interest which were made after the magic date of 1870 which he supports. Guns belonging, for example, to President Theodore Roosevelt and President Calvin Coolidge would be subject to this sort of control.

The stereotyped buyers of guns appear: juvenile delinquents, dope addicts, and mental defectives. And this despite laws which already exist rather adequately covering the purchase of such weapons before 1968. The point is that long before 1968, the overwhelming bulk of firearms purchases were made by responsible citizens for legitimate purposes. Mr. Kilpatrick's idea of what legitimate sportsment ought to want differs quite a bit from what they do want. What they do want, including the reduction of crime, will hardly be accomplished by his "ideal" bill.

## 5. WHAT ARE THE ATTACKS ON GUNS?

Opponents of private ownership of firearms would have us believe that guns are dangerous, the possessions of lunatics, and the weapons of the powers of darkness. Many of the proponents of firearms restrictions have what sportsmen often call the "Bambi complex," in that they see wildlife as it comes to life in a Walt Disney cartoon. The feel many times that guns increase crime, if only because thieves will steal them before they can be used for defense, thereby neeedlessly arming a thief. And, one suspects many times, they are proponents of big government and large bureaucracy who hope to see more governmental power through the control of one additional area of property. Finally, some are pacifists, who see the world through rose-colored glasses. If we had no weapons, individual or collective, specifically in the armies of the world, we would live together peacefully and profitably and fully. Let us examine briefly each of these objections and provide a commentary on each.

*The Bambi Complex.* Bambi, the reader will recall, was the subject of a full length cartoon feature film. Bambi and his friends, like the rabbit Thumper, lived in the pretty woods at peace with all other animals. They never got hungry, thirsty, cold or hunted. Once in a while a mean, dirty, nasty human being would do something foul, like start a forest fire or shoot one of the pretty animals. How dreadful. But what a beautiful picture if only it were true.

The conclusions to be drawn are obvious. Let Bambi and his nice friends alone, mean, old hunter. Go buy domestically slaughtered beef. Bambi and company will be very, very happy if left in the pretty forest. How could anyone slaughter a deer or a rabbit or a squirrel? Take away man's guns and he cannot do these terrible things. Educate men so that he need not undergo the ritual of manhood by killing like a savage.

Ah, if only this picture were true! But, alas, it is not. Bambi and friends are killed by automobiles. They starve to death by the thousands annually. They kill one another. Nature, in its "survival of the fittest" provides that only the strongest of each species lives. The rest must die. Some are killed by other animals. Some are tortured by slow deaths which are illogically prescribed by nonsensical laws, as, for example, after being injured by accident while most state laws allow such wild animals to be destroyed only by game wardens. And some are killed by hunters in pursuit or sport and meat.

Sportsmen have voluntarily contributed to funds established to repopulate endangered species. They have aided in the recovery of many species through such organizations as Ducks Unlimited. Their taxes, paid on ammunition and reloading components, whether used or not used for hunting, pay for game wardens, conservation officers, and wildlife breeding farms. A true sportsman does not kill young game animals. Most often he will choose to kill older animals or crippled animals who might not survive anyway. Many hunters voluntarily choose not to hunt species which are scarce in a given area, even if such hunting is legal.

In areas, such as certain national and state forests, sportsmen are barred. A victory for wildlife? Hardly. Species still die naturally. Professional hunters are hired, paid with tax dollars, to "thin out" the herds. And the carcasses are left to rot.

Endangered species seldom are brought to the brink of extinction by sportsmen. Ecological factors, such as poisons in the atmosphere, DDT and other chemicals in food and water supplies, destructions of natural habitats by construction, and the like are generally the culprits. Sportsmen are perhaps the most vocal group in our country concerning the protection of animal or bird life whose existence is in jeopardy.

*The Manhood Ritual.* Ian Flemming of James Bond fame may be credited with popularizing the "phallic symbol" argument in his last novel *Man with the Golden Gun*, in which hero Bond is given a lesson in psychology by headquarters before going out to capture the Man. The villian, Bond is told by the psychiatrist, fulfills his sexual role and/or inadequacy by having a fancy Colt .45 revolver. *Playboy*, which serialized this Bond story, picked up the tempo in subsequent anti-gun articles and comments.

There is no doubt that, in a culture which puts baby's first shoes in "lasting, permanent bronze on an oak plaque," there is a consequent bit of ritual in a boy's first shooting lesson, his first gun or his first game kill. Perhaps it is viewed as a more "manly" event than his first violin or ballet lesson. This we can readily admit. That it may historically parallel a knight's sword ritual, a primitive tribe's giving of a spear to a new hunter, or some such event we can also admit. But I cannot see how we can equate this event with a "manhood initiation rite" as performed, perhaps in the depths of the Congo.

105

One might trace this whole attitude back to Thorstein Veblen's bitter attack on society in *The Theory of the Leisure Class* in which this sociologist-economist equates all he does not like in society with one or another pagan ritual. It is barbaric, ergo it is evil. I think the best approach might well be to dismiss it without trying to line up a group of psychiatrists to testify to the contrary or some such thing. It is, at best, tenuous and hypotehtical, representing isolated opinion, which opinion is then mimicked into truth by those who are unaccredited to pass on its truth or falsehood.

*Guns Are Dangerous.* Like many other mechanical things, from power tools to snowmobiles, guns are potentially dangerous *in the hands of those who do not use them properly.* Of this there is no question. The question, however, is whether this is sufficient to "outlaw" guns. The owner of a gun *may* be injured using it, even while cleaning it. So may the owner or an outboard motor boat, a meatgrinder or an electric drill. An individual has a right to take a chance with his life if he chooses. Because some skydivers are killed, does this mean that society has the right to stop you from skydiving?

If one breaks down killings or injuries caused by firearms, one finds that the list of statistics usually given must be misleading. First, one cannot count injuries sustained by the owner of the gun in any meaningful way. If the owner brings harm to himself with his gun, that is the calculated risk which he obviously was willing to take. He could rationally reduce the chances by learning to use his gun properly.

Second, suicide is not desirable, it is most likely morally wrong (a sin), and it may be proper for society to attempt to prevent. Technically, it is a crime in most areas of the civilized world. But a gun is merely a handy device, which, in many cases, is used because it is efficient. It is highly unlikely that barring guns completely would affect suicide rates. Certainly, in the final analysis, this is a highly personal matter. It is also a matter which can be discussed in terms of its status as a crime. This writer does not believe that these statistics should be used to damn firearms ownership.

Third, crimes of passion, psychologically speaking, are caused by a state of mind in the would-be assailant. One of society's great unanswerable questions is how to prevent this sort of crime. If a way can be found to prevent this sort of crime, society would indeed be very near a utopian ideal, a secular millenium. Here, by very definition of the term "passion," there is no conscious planning, no prior contemplation, no logical reflection. There is only the instant demand for action. The tool to be used as a weapon *may* be a gun; but it may also be a knife, a golf club, or a piece of glass. If reflection were available a gun might be chosen, but this has been ruled out by definition. Even certain opponents of private firearms ownership readily acknowledge that lowering the incidence of available firearms would not tend to diminish this sort of crime appreciably, even at all.

Fourth, carefully planned and organized crime carried out by a highly organized conspiracy would in no tangible way be affected. The political assassination of a key figure, if planned by some major or international organization, would not disappear upon regulation of firearms. In John Frankenheimer's "The Manchurian Candidate" the would-be assassin carried a Russian sniper rifle of World War II vintage, presumably given him by the organization which controlled him. Guns can be smuggled into a country with ease if necessity dictates. Organized crime might find the importation of firearms, even their underground domestic manufacture, to be most expedient in case of total confiscation. If political assassination were the major obsession of an individual or group, a way to carry out such a plan would be found—with guns, explosives, even bow and arrow. The Sullivan Law in New York has not precluded young hoodlums from obtaining weapons, including homemade "zip guns."

This then leaves the simple premeditated crime, such as bank robbery or hold-ups of merchants, certain classes of premeditated murder and a few others to be subjected to our inquiry. Again, unfortunately for the anti-gun forces, little is to be gained here. In the first instance, penal legislation for the commission of crimes ought to be the deterrent. And, in the second instance, other weapons, including "dummy" guns, knives and explosives are an available alternative to real firearms. There ought to be more interest in education against crime. For example, in Pittsburgh, Pennsylvania, during 1971 the average "take" in a hold-up of a bank was less than $200. It is indeed strange to find a society in which a man is willing to risk so much for so little. There must be causes more basic than simple availability of firearms.

*The Mentality of Disarmament.* Many one worldists feel that if guns and all other weapons were to be confiscated and destroyed this world would be better off. There would be no wars, "police actions," "interventions," and, perhaps, no crime. We educate little children by buying them a toy gun. Now we all know guns are made only for killing. Television programs and movies tell us this. If we gave little boys innocuous toys and took away big boys guns then we could all live happily, peacefully and prosperously forever. A child not taught to kill in play will not kill as a man.

Certain plans offered at conferences such as the SALT talks and the Geneva Conference on Disarmament have suggested that civilians as well as the military be disarmed. Should a treaty be made in this fashion it might well contravene the Second Amendment. Precedent has been offered for this sort of thing in the case of the regulation of hunting migratory birds. The power to regulate bird hunting was reserved to the states until we entered into a treaty with other nations to regulate this hunting. Then it suddenly became constitutional; a treaty had overridden the Constitution.

The approach here is really two-fold. On the one side, we find the basic suggestion, offered by Lord Russell and others, that armaments have not kept us out of wars, therefore we ought to see how well disarmament works. On the other side, it is a reaction to the mentality that if one seeks peace he ought to prepare for war. They presume great good will by all other camps and a similar willingness to disarm and place one's hopes in the arena of peaceful adjudication of disputes. The other camps are just as afraid as we are, they reason, and if we show our good will first, and someone must go first, they will show equal good will. They presume that all countries are governed by rational men with honest intentions.

Like all other simplistic explanations, this one seeks to improve mankind's conditions by a very simple device: disarmament. Other philosophies have suggested that all ills could be cured by a wide variety of other monolithic devices, such as confiscation of all private property, forced compliance with a single universal religion, or universal dictatorships. Many would wish that such an alternative would work. There is, of course, little to go by in history to prove that it would not work. Still, there are a few parallels. After conflicts with Rome, for example, the people of ancient Carthage followed Roman directions to disarm, even gave up hostages to guarantee their survival and to show their good will. This did not prevent Rome from so destroying Carthage in a few years that nothing grew on that land for centuries. After World War 1, " the war to end all wars," major nations agreed to limit arms through the Pact of Paris (Kellogg-Briand Agreement) and other devices. All disputes were to be settled peacefully through world organization. Within a decade, dictatorships had broken these agreements and were arming as fast as technology permitted.

Breaking the back of civilian training would insure that our nation, or any nation, had no trained manpower available to rise up in defense of the state. Removing guns from the citizenry would remove all sources of resistance to internal or external tyranny. In a recent movie made for television, "Shadow Over the Land" a fascist-style dictatorship rises and the citizens resist. But, as usual, it was fictional for the citizens used automatic weapons to retain their freedom. Save for groups such as the Minutemen or organized crime, no such civilian weapons exist. Television not only goofs again; it creates a strange ambivalence: it condemns the para-military groups when they exist in the here and now, yet makes them heroes in times of need.

# WHY GUNS?

Political scientists, such as Inis Claude in his *Swords Into Plowshares*, speak of the value of collective security in which there is only a single retaliatory force headed up by international organization which will immediately recognize an aggressor, realize that a breech of the peace anywhere threatens all nations everywhere, and then act decisively to massively respond to that threat to mankind. Such a utopian system is so impractical that even proponents do not speak in terms of its applicability in the present in any serious way. When one speaks of defining the aggressor in such a contemporary incident as the recent Indian-Pakistani War or the Arab-Israeli War there is no consensus, even in this country, let alone all countries.

*Governmental Power and Regulation.* It may well be that the "war on poverty" is really not concerned with the poor, but, is rather concerned with the unemployed middle class college graduates. These people, sustained with tax dollars, are paid to do the work, real and unreal, necessary and unnecessary, of government. If one is in a position of command, he naturally seeks to acquire more power and a greater span of control. The greater bureaucracy, the more jobs there are for potential bureaucrats. Given an area such as firearms control, where there is a minimum of governmental control, there is the potential for a fantastic growth of power.

Therefore, in the name of reducing crime, a new bureaucracy is created. Clerks, secretaries, investigators, and administrators would be needed in large numbers. Files must be maintained, records kept, computers programmed and clients serviced. The cost would be enormous, perhaps as much as $200 million in the first year alone. The cost would be borne, ultimately, by the taxpayer, whether through a "service fee" or by the "general fund."

That the money may be better spent on more efficient law enforcement of better courts is unimportant. If the latter be true, we can, presumably, have both systems. That such a system of registration and/or licensing would not do the job for which it is intended is again unimportant, for the primary purpose is as stated, to create new bureaucratic jobs and power. This is not nearly so much an anti-firearms position as it is a pro-bureaucratic position.

In summary, then, if there is a psychological or pathological need for guns, there are similar proclivities which predispose other people to hate guns and all that they feel guns stand for. Because they do not like guns certain people feel that no one ought to like them or have them. The arguments of many, to be sure, are honest, although based on misplaced logic, misplaced emotion, or misguided information. The cleavage which has been consequent to the discourse on guns ownership has cut off communications on vital issues. The National Rifle Association, the National

Shooting Sports Foundation, or any other institution of the "guns establishment" do not wish to see crime increase or murders take place. On the issue of law and order versus crime they are on the same side as anti-guns spokesmen. They do not, cannot by any logic, bear the burden of guilt for any sort of crime. Criminals, after all, do the murders, rapes, robberies and so on. The problem lies in seeking answers to questions from wide and unrelated areas by those who do not know whereof they speak.

# FOOTNOTES

[1] New York *Times*, 4 September 1968.

[2] Washington *Post*, 7 June 1969.

[3] Washington *Star*, 29 June 1968.

# CHAPTER 9

## EMOTION AND FACT IN THE FIREARMS CONTROVERSY

Whereof One Cannot Speak
Thereof One Must Be Silent
*Ludwig Wittgenstein*

It is most unfortunate that the majority of writers who have condemned the private possession of firearms are blissfully ignorant; for one cannot argue with an individual who has no basis whatsoever in experience with those things which he is condemning. The author confesses a strong personal prejudice against motorcycles, but any attempt on his part to condemn them would be absolutely absurd since he has never been on one, has no ideas how one operates, etc. Yet in my discussions with the anti-firearms fraternity it is much the same case: they often have no idea how to load a gun, how to fire one, or what the limits on the dangers of firearms, ammunition and components therefore are. To make the statement that gunpowder is dangerous and explosive is one thing; to demonstrate the limits on that statement is yet another. The author will therefore presume that the reader knows little or nothing about firearms or about property rights, which two topics intertwine here.

## 1. IGNORANCE AND FIREARMS

The testimony received in steady doses by the Senate Committee on the Judiciary, Subcommittee to Investigate Juvenile Delinquency, during most of the 1960's dealth with the problems of the government in controlling mail order and very large calibre weapons. Until 1968, there were few state, and no national, controls over foreign imports, military surplus and large bore weapons. In short, a cannon could be ordered by almost anyone 18 years of age, and the government objected to this, seeking from Congress laws to stop this traffic. Presumably, an individual is to be frightened and run to the government for protection from any lunatic who would own anything larger than a .30 or .45 calibre weapon; or so the Senate hearings would have us believe.

In one of the classic scare cases of the twentieth century, the members of the Senate who opposed firearms gathered testimony from far and wide, argued by accusation and innuendo, and simply frightened the honest but uneducated citizen into believing that an invasion by the new nazis was imminent. What could anyone who was a law-abiding citizen want, they demanded, with a bazooka or a small cannon? Such an individual had to be a lunatic. There was no protected right whatsoever to maintain an arsenal which included anything other than antiques or regular sporting arms. This would be too much read into the non-existent right to bear arms. The National Rifle Association quickly accepted compromise: they would not accept total regulation, but maybe this time it would be well to negotiate. They would accept a policy of appeasement to forestall total controls. So the NRA accepted controls over large bore, modern weapons. And it accepted the limitations imposed on weapons of foreign military origin. And the drive for total registration was halted for the time being.

How dangerous were the big bore weapons? There is absolutely no question that such weapons are potentially dangerous, for, with regular ammunition, they are just like a regular rifle only several times more powerful, shooting with several times the force and carrying for perhaps several times the distance. For all intents and purpose they have no sporting use; i.e., hunting known species of game. With explosive, incindiary, and tracer ammunition they are quite a bit more dangerous, for seldom does any of that sort of thing turn up on the retail market for sale to shooters of smaller arms. Certainly, there can be a case made out for simply outlawing explosive and incindiary ammunition and for limiting and closely supervising tracers.

Let us approach the subject this way: suppose an adult has an interest in owning a 20mm recoiless rifle simply for his own pleasure and perhaps to shoot ten times a year in a deserted part of the country. Is it the proper function of government to deny him this right, to confiscate or severely tax with an eye at confiscating his property? We are supposing that, like the overwhelming bulk of the owners of large bore guns, our shooter here has never violated any law in regard to the use of his weapon. He has always provided adequate background to stop his shots without damage; he has used "straight" ammunition in it; he has transported it safely; and he has stored it out of the reach of those unfit to use it. Is this any case to condemn?

It hardly seems probable that a felon intent on robbing a store is going to buy and use a several hundred pound cannon; or that a group bent on civil revolution is going to use such a weapon when "molotov cocktails" and other devices which can be made simply and portably are readily available. There is no doubt concerning the potential danger of a cannon or large bore weapon similar to a cannon, but it would seem that such danger has been overrated. Since the shells usually cost a minimum of $1 each, it hardly seems like the sort of weapon that would attract the average shooter. Perhaps it would be better that society tolerate such ownership than restrict it. There is no available statistical information which would indicate that any sort of crime could be restrained or lessened by confiscating and outlawing all such weapons. Even crime involving such weapons exclusively may not be lessened because it has happened many times that such weapons were stolen from military bases. The policy of limitations on these big bore weapons seems to flow from the personal imperative of its supporters, that people should not have these weapons because they are not the sort of weapons people should have. After such circular logic what response can be given?

The Senate Committee hearings most often contained a large number of pictures of advertisements for these large bore weapons.[1] One is presumably supposed to look at these pictures, recoil in horror and conclude that no normal red-blooded American boy could possibly want to own such an object. By the same logic one might show one of the current crop of distended racing cars and conclude that since it does not look like a 1949 Ford it cannot be useful.

More dangerous yet to American sportsment was the ban on the importation of foreign-made and foreign-used military weapons. The hysteria over the assassination of President John Kennedy in 1963 set off a strong wave of anti-gun sentiment, culminating, eight years later, in a highly restrictive piece of legislation. It was obvious from that day in November 1963 onward that one certain casualty of the impending legislation would be the foreign-made or foreign-used weapon, for the gun associated with the Kennedy assassination was an Italian army rifle which might have been used in any phase of Italy's involvement in World War II. Certainly a weapon inferior to virtually anything else made in the twentieth century, it was not the most desirable weapon to import for it had certain unhandy features, notably the safety, and ammunition which was reliable was difficult to procure. Still, the price was right, usually under $15 and often under $10, and it wholesaled around $2, making it popular to buyers and sellers. It was reasonably reliable with good ammunition, despite the necessity of clip loading, and quite rugged.

The author would like to make several remarks here pertinent to the imported rifle which killed President Kennedy. First, it was procured illegally under statutes already on the books, meaning of course that the recipient should have been prevented from ever acquiring the weapon in the first place if legislation is viewed as being the cure for such crimes. Second, if this writer were ever going to be the object of violence, he

113

would hope that his would-be killer would select a weapon such as the Italian carbine rather than a modern, American made weapon. Third, this author has never been able to accept the contention of the Warren Commission that the Italian carbine was the one and only weapon used in the assassination. My own guess at that time was that an M-1 carbine had been used if only one individual was involved. My feelings against the supposed weapon are still the same today.

A grieved nation sought something to prevent this sort of thing from ever happening again. So it struck out against the inanimate object which had been the tool of the assasin: the imported gun. To be sure this type of weapon had been under fire already. Certain manufacturers felt the pressures of competition and supported the anti-guns contingents in Congress. The five years preceeding the assassination had seen the importation of many surplus weapons from overseas, some good, some not good, but all quite inexpensive. Some were American weapons sent over during World War II; some were more recent additions to the arsenals of our allies.

The good weapons included: Colt and Smith & Wesson handguns, most of which had been sent to Britain and her colonies during one of the world wars; German made Mauser 98 rifles, standard in both world wars, and the basis for many a custom rifle in the United States as well as a rifle used "as is" with readily available U.S. made ammunition; German Lugers and Walther P-38s, perhaps the most famous and best loved handguns in the world; American M-1 Garands, used in national match shooting, and a fine weapon given as surplus to our allies after World War II; and English made Enfields, U.S. made Enfields and Springfields, the mainstays of American and British armies for decades, quite usable "as is" or convertible for sporting use.

More marginal items included French, Swedish, Danish, Spanish, and Swiss army rifles, each with strength, reliability and safety, but each with difficulties in respect to availability of parts, ammunition or convertability for sporting use. In addition to rifles, importers offered handguns from these nations. In addition to these more common weapons, importers made available to collectors some of the more esoteric firearms of exotic places like Siam, Indonesia and Burma. Many of these firearms found their way into collections and would never be fired again, while other collectors enjoyed having a moderately priced collection of weapons which could be safely fired.

I believe that it can be argued convincingly that weapons were offered to individuals who hitherto could not afford a firearm for hunting and sporting purposes at prices which would have otherwise been impossible. Further, the majority of these weapons were safer than what might have been procured domestically for twice the price. There are many rural families who cannot afford both a rifle and a shotgun so the youngster generally hunts only with a single barrel shotgun for all game. A $10 British Enfield would serve him well for his hunting until he could afford a decent gun.

I doubt whether the enemies of firearms have ever seen a young man take his $10 Mauser and lovingly strip it down, discard that old military stock, put on a new semi-finished blank stock, and, over an entire winter, refinish it so that it literally glistens. Some would just take off the old finish from the military stock, which may have seen action the world over, and put a new coat over it so it looks like new. I doubt also if they have ever seen a master gunsmith take a German 98 Mauser and completely strip it, install a new barrel, reblue it, alter the safety so that it can be used with a telescopic sight, install a $100 stock, checker that stock and come out with one of the most beautiful rifles ever seen by man. Some of this nation's finest and most accurate weapons have as their base a war surplus action.

American industry certainly has profited from this activity as have America's sportsmen. The wood industries which supply new replacement gunstocks, the sight manufacturers and scope manufacturers, makers of custom safeties and triggers, and the ammunition manufacturers all benefit. Many shooters then engage in reloading ammunition, buying additional accessories and so on, which again feed money into the economy. So that in toto, very little of the money goes into foreign exchange all things considered. And very few of these weapons are simply stacked away to be used for bank holdups, revolutions or whatever illegal use one might suggest. In fact there is no statistical evidence available to show that there is a greater probability for misuse of these weapons than newly manufactured domestic weapons, despite the fact that these weapons on the surface are far and away more suitable for such misuse. However, as we shall show statistically, the index of misuse of firearms per number known to exist; i.e., the rate of firearm misuse, is very small indeed. The only class of firearm for which a high index of misuse can be shown is the illegally manufactuered firearm, e.g., the "zip gun." Military weapons which are imported for sale in the United States are very seldom "cut down" for use as hold-up weapons. Few are even semi-automatic and only one semi-automatic, the Russian Tokarev, is even remotely adaptable for automatic fire. In short, these weapons are good sporting equipment but very bad criminal weapons.

The last major area of weapons which are dramatically affected by recent legislation are newly manufactured foreign weapons. This class may be viewed as representing, as of, say, 1968, both the best and the worst of the firearms maker's art. At the top are the fine British and German

115

weapons which are truly the gunmaker's finest hour. These guns, usually double barrel shotguns, may run into $5,000 or more and involve a waiting period of up to five years for completion. At the bottom were the so-called "Saturday night specials," cheap firearms as once domestically manufactured c.1900 are the lowest type of article imported at the present time. Many were subject to safety deficiencies so severe as to jeopardize the shooter the first time he pulled the trigger. These pistols made with "pot metal" were not suitable in any way for sporting use, self-defense or hunting. Most appeared in calibre .22 rimfire, generally considered a target or small-game cartridge. Many could be broken by hand in several pieces; some would shake apart while firing, and none were accurate. All were dangerous in varying degrees. As we shall see in the chapter dealing with interstate commerce, the exclusion of these items is clearly within the purview of federal power.

In between the finest and the dangerous foreign imports is a whole class of weapons paralleling American domestic production. They might be direct copies of American weapons, such as the popular "Single Action Army" Cole revolver ("the gun that won the West") or novel productions, such as the German Walther automatic pistols. They may be foreign licensed variations on American productions or they may be specialty items. Many "American" firearms manufactuers have some or all of their production in other countries, attesting to the proficiency of certain foreign manufacturers.

It is quite correct therefore to have legislation which would limit the types of weapons imported into the United States to those which can be shown to have value for recreation, hunting and self-defense. The Congress has created minimum standards for safety and a point system to test the value of imported weapons under the 1968 legislation. Sportsmen may wish to question the precise criteria used, however, and to have provisions altered which in effect condemn all obsolete military weapons.

## 2. HANDLOADING AND IGNORANCE

Ignorance of legislative matters is not confined, in the weapons field, to the weapons themselves. It is associated with the reloading of ammunition to be fired in sporting and hunting arms. Many shooters find that they can afford to participate in their favorite sport to a far greater extent if they choose to reload empty shell casings. This is a very safe and interesting use of leisure time in and of itself. Costs of shooting can be decreased as much as 75% by making one's own bullets and then assembling primers, powders and bullet with the fired casing. In light loads in pistols, cases last almost indefinitely, making the cost slight. Since casings are generally brass at times coated with nickle, this helps reduce waste in semi-precious metal. It is, so to speak, a form of recycling that can be completed at home. Many shooters will even recycle lead in bullets.

The principal objections heard here are in regard to the storage of gunpowder and primers. Gunpowder is of course an explosive and in its original form (black powder) was quite dangerous. However, modern smokeless powders are far and away less dangerous than, say, gasoline. They are only flammable not explosive when unconfined, as in storage. They are not good explosives for revolutionaries to use, with molotov cocktails (made with gasoline) being much more useful to such individuals. Primers are not useful for anything beyond that for which they were designed, namely, setting off gunpowder in a shell casing. Of major "popular" explosives, gunpowder is probably the one with the least potential for bombs, etc. Even common nitrogen based fertilizers have greater potential. Handbooks seem to have been made readily available to the interested public in book form, even reprinting in extremist newspapers, which explain how to make dangerous explosives.[2] In such publications seldom is gunpowder mentioned as a source of explosive powder.

In certain states and communities reloaders have been subjected to severe restrictions in their attempts to obtain reloading components. For example, the city council of Oyster Bay, New York, passed, in 1967, an ordinance which prohibited the sale, transportation or possession of ammunition or reloading components without a license. The license which costs $10 per year must be approved by the police department. This ordinance restricts the collecting of cartridges as well.[3] This is a new area of control not touched hitherto by any level of government. New York State later pre-empted this field through a state bill which licenses reloaders. Other states have followed suit and additional jurisdictions have proposed similar legislation.

In August 1969, a bill was offered to Wisconsin Governor Milliken for his signature which would have required all handloaders to obtain police permits before purchasing black or smokeless powders. Calling this bill an "undue burden on sportsmen" Governor Milliken vetoed it. Sportsmen who had seen this bill pass the state legislature on 7 July 1969 had written to the Governor explaining that it would be of little value in curbing crime while subjecting the legitimate sportsman to unreasonable controls.[4] It is interesting to note that the state legislature did not pass the bill over the Governor's veto.

The tragedy of the proposals which have sought to control firearms components is that they are often based on the assumption that gunpowder is to be blamed for explosions which might be properly traced to their

117

causes. For example, Indiana attempted to introduce severe restrictions on the storage of powder and ammunition after a 1968 explosion killed 41 persons at Richmond. Even firearms opponent Senator Vance Hartke was of the opinion in a July interview that the true cause of the explosion was natural gas, not gunpowder. When the Richmond *Graphic* newspaper and the Richmond Board of Works had requested an investigation of the incident by the Indiana Public Service Commission, it got only a set of suggested restrictive guidelines on the storage of gunpowder and ammunition.[5]

As 1971 closed, Ohio considered the passage of restrictive legislation on the subject of ammunition and handloading. Persons over 21 who are Ohio residents who meet certain other requirements would be permitted to obtain an annual $10 Ohio Explosives License from the Department of Industrial Relations. This would allow them to buy up to 15 pounds of gun powder. They would of course be required to keep full records on the disposition of these explosives.[6]

That these bills fail is seen in the case of New York State. The bill there had required license costing $2.50 annually which allowed an individual to purchase up to 10 pounds of powder per year. When the bill failed, as sportsmen had maintained it would from the beginning, to reduce incidences of bombings, and when investigation of these bombings revealed they did not involve gunpowder generally, the legislation was repealed in April 1971.[7]

There is no real and effective way to trace small quantities of gunpowder. Like gasoline, much is consumed by many, and, of course, it may be stored in quantity with ease for a long time if reasonable precautions are observed. Blackpowder is easily manufactured, although this procedure can be dangerous to the novice. Because of its greater explosive quality, some controls over the storage of blackpowder may be dictated. However, this is not true of smokeless powder.

Taken in a simple way, one can look at handloading in this fashion: there are 7000 grains in a pound. Many rifle cartridges use about 50 grains per cartridge. Given a 50 or 15 pound limit, handloaders are severely limited unless they resort to the semi-legal device of having non-loaders purchase powder for them. Additionally, an individual may reload for his rifle, his shotgun, and pistol. Assuming that he has only three guns for which to load he must buy three types of powder. Any shooter who reloads much finds it economical to buy in quantity. It would not be unusual for a handloader to use as much as 20 pounds of powder in a year for shotgun or rifle alone. If an individual loads, say, for .30/30 rifle, a .30-06 rifle, a 12 guage shotgun and a .38 pistol, he probably would want to have a minimum of 5 kinds of powder on hand at all times. If he buys his shotgun powder in containers of 12½ or 20 pounds, he already has a fair amount of powder on hand at any given time. Is this in and of itself a danger or an evil? No chemist I have spoken to at my University would say yes.

The same is true for ammunition. Allowing that no one would keep any sizeable quantity of explosive, incindiary or tracer ammunition on hand, quantity in and of itself is of little consequence or concern to the state. It may be assumed that no individual has use for a million rounds of ammunition within a foreseeable time period, and that most shooters will have only 100 rounds at a given time, what constitutes a reasonable quantity? Is the control of, or inquiry into, this quantity the reasonable business of state, local or federal governments?

One reads an indictment by the press of a "lunatic" for keeping several thousand rounds of ammunition in his home and the audience is supposed to agree that only one mentally deranged or incompetent would want "several thousand rounds" in his home at a time. But is this the way of things? Is there quantitative guilt here? Does this mean that the person possessing a quantity of ammunition is readying for revolution or civil war? Some reloaders, including this writer, will load several thousand rounds each of pistol and rifle cartridges in two or three calibres during the winter for his shooting pleasure during the summer. Add to this a few hundred "miscellaneous" rounds for his other rifles, his cartridge type collection and a few thousand rounds of .22 ammunition, we are already well over the "several thousand" rounds of ammunition so offensive to the press. All to say nothing of shotgun shells stored away, awaiting the trap and skeet season. I know, as do most shooters, trap and skeet champions who shoot a few hundred rounds a week, every week, and a few hundred more in a contest or championship shootoff.

## 3. CONCLUSIONS

The conclusions to be drawn from this portion of our treatise are simple. First, hysteria, always a poor excuse for legislating anywhere, has been particularly damaging to the shooter and reloader. Second, more expertise and less emotion is needed when considering or proposing any legislation in this area. Third, the vast majority of bills regarding firearms harm only the legitimate sportsman and citizen, not the criminal. Fourth, these bills generally represent the worst in restricting property rights without reference to what property is involved. They restrict the property rights of the private, law-abiding citizen without promising him any protection or right in return. Property rights are fundamental to the protection and maintenance of a free, democratic republic and may be violated only for due cause, which cause is not evident here. Fifth, the idea of a maximum amount of property which can be possessed by a citizen is an exceedingly dangerous one in a capitalistic system such as ours. Sixth, the assumption of "facts" without sufficient evidence of their veracity is again dangerous to our system. Notable here is the assumption that all foreign military surplus firearms are junk and hence should be excluded.

The idea of licensing reloaders is particularly odious. If one is to infer logic in the arguments of the legislators who would license reloaders whose reloading is done as a hobby and not for profit, one can then find logic in an argument that all hobbies may be licensed. Allowing that there is a certain, even if very small, danger herewith associated, one can at least infer that licensing may be licit in at least other hobbies associated with some element of danger. Hence, one can license model airplane operators who deal with explosive fuels, campers who use matches, racing drivers who might run off the track or have their fuels blow up, and so on. This author recalls how strongly the press reacted in Pittsburgh when Mayor Flaherty suggested that members of the press be required to carry $10 licenses to practice their professions. Using their great power on radio and television and in the written press, this action was universally condemned by the fraternity. One can agree in spirit, but one wonders whether the gun owning fraternity could do away will all licensing and registration permits if it had the power of the press at its instant disposal.

## FOOTNOTES

[1] See, for example, The Hearings Before the Subcommittee to Investigage Juvenile Delinquency of the Committee on the Judiciary, pursuant to S. Res. 63, Part 14, Interstate Traffic in Mail-Order Firearms, January 29 and 30; March 7, and May 1 and 2, 1963, Washington, D.C.

[2] For example, publications such as those of the National Youth Alliance (NYA) *Attack* and others whose group affiliation is less obvious have run similar articles. Armed forces technical manuals have been reprinted which explain how to make even mines, plastic explosives and so on.

[3] New York *Times*, September 19, 1967.

[4] See *Gun Week,* 5 September 1969.

[5] See *Gun Week,* October 4, 1968; also the Richmond *Graphic*, issues of July 1969.

[6] See Pittsburgh *Press* and *Post-Gazette*, 22 December 1971, also *Gun Week*, 24 December 1971.

[7] See New York *Times*, April 30, 1971.

# CHAPTER 10

## THE POSITIVE APPROACH

Firearms ownership like any other right involves certain responsibilities. The mature firearm owner does not maintain that he has absolute property rights as he recognizes that no right is absolute. There are several steps which he can take rationally to incorporate his ideas into public policy. These are for the most part long range and continuing programs. For each use we can find for the right to keep and bear arms we can find corresponding ways to make this right more meaningful, safe and significant.

The first and perhaps most important step is education. It is an old chestnut that there is no substitute for education. There are several steps in the educational program which must be considered. To many sportsmen the first and most logical step is education for the general public concerning the right itself. The gun enthusiast will try to show the historical antecedents of the right, its importance today and its future applications. He will try to build his public relations contacts and show by example the correct use of guns. It is worth repeating that the misuse of firearms by one individual can undermine the good done by many others.

Speakers for firearms use are being seen more often today. The use of television to show the correct use of firearms is a fine positive step in this direction. Public displays and films are another way the sportsman can get his message across. Gun shows, especially of antique and historically related guns are growing throughout the country. Many of these shows previously were gatherings of dealers and collectors with the major purposes being commercial and social among a tightly knit fraternity. A bad public image was created at some gun shows by having tables laden with nazi medals, flags and other unrelated items. This sort of thing does little to convince the public that firearms collectors are not fascists.

The major educational program probably would be the use of school facilities to teach shooting sports. Most high schoolers are required to take a course in safety education. Instructors should teach, as an integral part of that course, firearms safety. Students should be taught how to handle firearms, how to check a gun to see if it is loaded and what the various characteristics of the various types of guns are. Instructors could be schooled in the teaching of firearms education, just as they learn any new program, by the function of universities called continuing education. In setting up the syllabus for the course of instruction the teacher could allow a week of instruction in this area.

The National Rifle Association of America and other local and state sportsmen's organizations have already created hunter safety programs which have to date graduated millions of school-aged children from such courses on a voluntary basis. Many states now require such instruction as a prerequisite for the issuance of a hunting license for youths. Adult education classes have enjoyed minor succes along the same lines. According to recent reports, the major difficulty encountered in creating adult or youth classes has been the lack of qualified instructors and suitable facilities. The addition of firearms safety programs in high school curricula would not be necessarily designed to replace voluntary programs carried on by public service or sportsmen's organizations. It should be noted that this is a long range program, the effect of which could not be immediately measured. It might serve to remove the inordinate fear held by some for any firearm. And, conversely, it could create proper respect for firearms by showing their potential power and destructiveness. Certainly, the instruction would create no obligation on the part of the student to own or use firearms any more than basic automobile safety creates a necessity for car ownership. And it need not require that a student fire a gun any more than automobile safety requires a student to actually drive a car.

A second phase of the education program deserves most serious attention. It is proposed here that as an integral part of the high school and college physical education programs shooting sports be included. Physical facilities should be created and made available to students on the same, equal basis that other aspects of physical education are made available. Qualified instruction should be provided just as for other sports. The minor premise of the argument for physical education has already been granted; that some physical activity is just as necessary as mental activity in high school and college curricula. What form of physical activity conventionally provided—basketball, football, wrestling, gymnastics, track and field, and so on—is best has long been argued. Generally, the allocation of sports activities has not been as important as the fact that sports are provided. The major premise of the argument here is that the paramount importance of shooting sports as related to national defense has been shown above. The conclusion then would be that the establishment of a national shooting sports education program is highly desirable.

If the argument advanced here is true then it would logically follow that we should find similar patterns of educational programming elsewhere as other nations and groups ought to have discovered the verity of this sort of argumentation. The communist countries have long had shooting sports training programs. The Soviet Union has a major and extensive program in its factories and communes. Workers are encouraged to learn to use weapons both of military and sporting types. Small bore (principally .22 calibre rimfire) ranges are found in many Soviet factories. Workers, after completing their shifts, can enjoy an evening of shooting for less than the equivalent of one U.S. dollar. The best rifles are provided and ammunition is quite inexpensive. A worker who does well is encouraged to shoot often and, if his progress is satisfactory, he can be sent to special schools for concentrated training, be transferred to factories or farms close to the best shooting ranges and be given a reduction in working hours to enable him to practice daily. Special ranges are created to simulate Olympic conditions as winning shooting events in the Olympic games is important to the Soviet Union. There are of course no professional athletes in the Soviet Union and since excellent shooters are in effect subsidized by the state, the Soviet Union has done very well in Olympic and other competition.

It is very important to note that the Soviet shooters are rarely directly connected with the Red Army. Rather, they seem almost to prefer that their competitive shooters be civilians. And, by the same token, the shooting competition carried on in fields and factories is not done in, through or under the auspices of the Red Army. The intelligent observer, however, can see the military implications of a prepared, able shooting population. At times the Soviet Union uses military weapons for its civilian shooting programs. Two items here are noteworthy. First, there are, for all intents and purposes, no "civilian" arms produced in the U.S.S.R. The .22 calibre weapons generally are quite similar to the large bore regular military rifles and, when used, pistols. The civilian shooter then has had experience with guns which have the same "feel" and handling qualities as the Russian military weapons. Second, the government arsenals need tool up for the production principally of only two types of cartridges: training and military. There is here no "switch over" time required. In the United States most of the civilian shooters use cartridges other than those used by the army.

In Red China, most civilians are in effect members of the "People's Militia" and consequently virtually all of the population has had some weapons training. Civilian weapons here are virtually unknown as in the U.S.S.R. Chinese factories and communes emphasize complete firearms training. Most Chinese have been instructed in the care and maintenance of the AK-47, the principal weapon of the Chinese People's Liberation Army. Like the Russians, the Red Chinese underwrite the cost of these training programs. The same is generally true of Fidel Castro's Communist Cuba.

123

The effectiveness of this firearms training program, a well-armed and trained population and the people's militia was shown in the Invasion at the Bay of Pigs.

The Cubans and Chinese, and, to a slightly lesser degree, the Russians train their people with automatic weapons. As the modern armies use fully automatic weapons, this program makes sense. The people who shoot in the United States have no access to automatic weapons for all intents and purposes. Citizens cannot own their own guns, with a few exceptions in the U.S.S.R. such as hunters or trappers. However, this is not surprising for two reasons. First, private property of all sorts is not a communist institution regardless of the type of private property. Secondly, after training the people these totalitarian countries are not about to allow the people to have the wherewithal to overthrow these dictatorships.

One may note, too, that both fascist Europe and totalitarian Japan had similar education programs for firearms training. Fascist Italy and Japan manufactured miniature military weapons for training the young in grade and high schools. Nazi Germany had military-style drill with tools before weapons were widely available. Most countries intent on world or regional conquest historically have trained their citizens with the available weapons of the times.

It may be objected that only totalitarian systems train their population with arms. Democratic systems, it has been argued, do not need such training and education. With approaching world government and the impossibility of another world war, it has been held, we need to disarm rather than prepare our population for the use of weapons. It would therefore be valuable to examine these arguments in detail.

The most extensive firearms training program in the world would be Switzerland's universal military training. A few other countries have systems of universal military training as well, notably Finland. While one can certainly overemphasize the value of this training in respect to the freedom enjoyed by these democracies, it is one factor which would be properly noted in assessing their freedom. Geography has played a pivotal role in both Finland and Switzerland. Still, the defense the heroic Finns maintained against Soviet aggression in the early months of the Second World War kept them free. Virtually every man in a Finnish town was prepared to defend his home with his gun. Switzerland was not overrun by either the Nazis or the Soviets, but one reason certainly would have to be the potential defense of Swiss marksmen of their mountain home.

Being prepared, as the Swiss have been for many years, does not mean that eventually this preparation must be put to the ultimate test in action. A man, regardless of nationality, who can use a gun need never fire a shot in anger. How a gun will be used depends a great deal more on other factors than it depends on the preparedness of the owner. Total education, including firearms education, may be the primary key to the reduction of war and violence. Since there may be legitimate uses of firearms other than the killing of men, the man who is so prepared may use his knowledge for these other purposes.

Colleges, universities and high schools can easily add a few courses in shooting sports. Technical and trade schools could additionally add such training without great difficulty. One can see great use for shooting sports training in certain programs in every level of education. A student who might be interested in a career in law enforcement could certainly make use of such training. The same is true of careers in forestry, wildlife management and outdoor recreation. If a safety education program is to be instituted then at least some student teachers would need such courses. Presumably pre-officer training programs for the military do now use and will continue to use such courses of instruction. Scholarships now provided in abundance for other athletics which allow young men and women to attend college, when otherwise they might not, could be created for shooting sports. As many physically handicapped individuals cannot compete in other athletics, shooting sports could provide for many a meaningful alternative to such contemporary physical education courses as ball room dancing, golf, tennis or badminton.

The Winchester-Western division of Olin Mathieson Chemical Corporation has been a real leader in the area of development of college-related shooting programs. Currently there are over 200 American colleges and universities participating in shooting sports as a regular part of their physical education or student activities programs. Winchester-Western has been most instrumental in helping to create these programs. Curriculum includes air-gun training, trap and skeet and small-bore riflemanship. The National Student Committee for the Right to Bear Arms has as a part of its program the institution of shooting sports related activities on college campuses. Many Reserve Army Training training programs offer scholarships to students for riflemanship. Most ROTC programs have competitive rifle shooting teams on college campuses. Such existing shooting ranges could easily serve as the nucleus of expanded shooting sports activities.

Adult education has been expanding rapidly in the United States, with various colleges and universities offering training "off-campus." Taking cue from these activities, many other organizations have begun offering adult education classes in hobbies, sports and recreational activities. Shooting sports have just begun to explore the possibilities here. A few progressive communities have found sponsors among sportsmen's groups for adult instruction in using firearms. Special classes have been created in the use of weapons for self-defense, often with the police or sheriff's office

125

providing the facilities and the bulk of the instruction. Such programs offer much potential for the future.

Special classes have been created for women or for businessmen or for shopkeepers, especially in areas with high rates of crimes of violence. Additional classes have been offered especially for women in hunting skills. Some sports shop owners have found clinics dealing with the reloading of ammunition quite profitable in several ways. Many persons who once had fear of gunpowder kept by reloaders found that it was far less dangerous than they had at first believed. Additional persons who had once never thought of handloading as a recreational activity were attracted.

Youth programs seem to be logically at the core of any education program. New York youths once roaming the streets were brought into shooting classes by a small group of sportsmen. They were in effect a test group. Of over 100 boys brought into the program not one misued the knowledge he gained by belonging to the shooting club. General comments found that the boys had begun to act more responsibly, had fewer scrapes with police and did better in school. Much of this may logically be attributed to the fact that men payed attention to them without regard to what type of activity was conducted. But they did take an interest in the care, use and maintenance of their equipment.

This is but one of many examples which could be given of the legitimate use of firearms education programs in the community. It can be presumed that many objects, guns certainly included, are misused because the possessor does not know how to use them properly. With over 10 million knowledgeable gun owners at a minimum in the United States this is indeed correctable ignorance in regard to guns.

Community action programs always seem to be looking for legitimate recreation activities for young and old alike. The story is told that basketball originated because someone was looking for an indoor sport which could be played with a minimum of equipment in a confined space. Certainly these requisites are present in the shooting sports save for trap and skeet. Even here air-powered or $CO_2$ powered skeet and trap promise to move these sports indoors. Certainly shooting sports know no age limitations. An old hall can be transformed into a shooting range. Minimum equipment would include only targets, a bullet trap and several small-bore rifles.

The growth of shooting sports can be seen in the success of Winchester-Western's franchised trap and skeet clubs. Principally located near urban areas, these clubs offer instruction by professionals, expert advice on the selection of equipment and accessories and an opportunity to try the sport before making any purchase. Other non-franchised shooting clubs are growing as well.

The Boy Scouts of America, as well as other youth organizations, been quite active with regard to shooting sports. A merit badge has long been offered for marksmanship in the Boy Scout movement. Most scout camps offer instruction in shooting as a part of their regular schedule. National Rifle Association junior marksmanship training has been very successful, although activities here have been damaged to some degree by the government's recent refusal to continue its long-standing full support. This program, with its excellent safety record, was damaged in the post-1963 wave of gun hysteria. Numerous boys have learned—and still learn—basic firearms safety and handling through the NRA programs. A series of enticements through marksmanship awards are offered to participants making this a desirable program for boys to continue.

## THE POSITIVE APPROACH: PHASE II

It is not the thesis of this book that the right to keep and bear arms is unlimited. On the contrary, throughout the book, we will be noting a series of limitations on this right. The courts long have agreed that Americans cannot simply expect to be able to walk out carrying any weapon in any manner into any place he desires. Although rights in the First Amendment have expanded beyond belief in many ways, it is our purpose here to consider a bar minimum of acceptable standards for the enforcement of the Second Amendment. This writer doubts if the Second Amendment to the Constitution will ever be given the widest latitude in meaning accorded to its companion amendments.

The Constitution clearly provided for "full faith and credit" to be extended to rights and privileges granted to citizens of one state by another. Nevertheless, the enforcement of "full faith and credit" has consistently provided more than a small amount of trouble for citizens. State $A$ may refuse to recognize a "junior" driver's license issued by state $B$; the same is true of marriage-divorce proceedings and other legal operations. Nowhere has this been more than with regard to the ownership, possession and transportation of firearms. In a survey done in conjunction with the preparation of the manuscript of this book, no state responded that it would uncategorically recognize any firearm permit issued by another state. Several Western states responded that they "generally" would not "bother" a person transporting a firearm in compliance with the law—whatever that means. A few states, mostly in the Southwest, noted they would honor permits on a reciprocal basis. None indicated any states with whom they have reciprocal compacts or agreements. When speaking less formally "off the record" police officers, that is, those directly concerned with the actual day-to-day enforcement of the law, noted that circumstances would play a large role in determining whether an out-of-stater was carrying firearms legally. A few officers candidly admitted "off the record" that racial considerations as well as those of the appearance of the possessor would play a significant role in their action or inaction. Presumably, a white middle class citizen who appeared "average" would then be able to do what, hypothetically, a black with an Afro haircut could not do.

Some states simply have no provision for the issuance of firearms permits for their own citizens let alone out-of-staters. Most states issuing permits have no provision for even temporary permits for non-citizens. One state, South Carolina, seems to have outlawed handguns totally, although this writer can attest to having seen such weapons sold openly. Some states require permits even to possess or carry rifles and shotguns while others simply control the transportation of concealed weapons. Added to this is a maze of local legislation. It has been estimated that upwards of 5000 or more jurisdictions have some regulation concerning the owning, possessing or carrying of weapons. A few states have largely pre-empted control, but even in these cases special permission may be granted by the state legislature to some minor jurisdiction.

## HOW TO BEAR ARMS?

Against this background, it has become a guessing game and perhaps even a risk game for the gun owner who may have some legitimate reason for wishing to carry a weapon in interstate commerce. In cases where there is no state pre-emption and/or permit system transit in even intrastate commerce can be difficult. The most desirable way to rectify this situation would be for the United States Supreme Court to set acceptable minimal standards which would limit all jurisdictions with regard to the Second Amendment. Second, one or more of the various proposals for uniform state laws, at least with respect to basic rights, might one day be universally adopted. Third, the federal courts might begin true enforcement of the "full faith and credit" clause of the U.S. Constitution. Let us now examine each of these in turn.

The first alternative of judicial review of the Second Amendment has been discussed above. We have already stated a strong prejudice in favor of the court's doing its duty by the Constitution. This would not in and of itself be sufficient, for there might be legitimate reason for carrying a weapon in excess of the constitutionally guaranteed minimum protection of the right to bear arms. Certainly, the Supreme Court of the United States cannot long continue to refuse to state the full and complete meaning of the Second Amendment.

128

The second proposal is at one and the same time a bit utopian and perhaps not desirable. The same laws overall might not fit the entire nation. It hardly seems practical to suggest that after decades of diversity we would suddenly find incorporation of such a uniform system of laws. Finally, only one state would have to refuse to accept such a system to have it fail. It is doubtful if the federal government would ever force such uniformity and additionally such an event would violate the system of divided sovereignty upon which our federal system is built.

The third proposal is meaningful and certainly should come about ideally as it is a constitutional mandate. Nevertheless, the enforcement of the "full faith and credit" clause would do nothing in the event that either the state of residence had no provision for issuing a permit or the state in which one was traveling had no permit system. Again, it is not broad enough to cover all possibilities which might arise; and it would be dependent upon the continued support by the courts of the "full faith and credit" clause and the continued existence of both states' permits systems, which, presumably, could be easily withdrawn by act of the state legislature. Finally, there are still the problems of exceptions to general state legislation by local jurisdictions. For example, a New York state permit from another area may not be honored in New York City.

## PLACING THE BLAME IN THE RIGHT PLACE

No sportsman, hunter or gun fancier wishes to see unlimited use or misuse of firearms. These men have long favored placing the blame in the right place: the man who abuses his right to keep and bear arms. The National Rifle Association, the National Committee for the Right to Bear Arms, the National Shooting Sports Foundation and all other known pro-guns organizations have long sought to create legislation which would punish the criminal for misusing the gun. Such legislation has generally supported creating a mandatory additional penalty for the misuse of a firearm during the commission of a felony.

Many states have created such legislation, but the courts have been reluctant to impose the optional additional penalty for using a firearm while committing a felony. The recent survey done in connection with this book indicates that percentages of use of such additional penalties run less than 1%. Even in states and other jurisdictions where the penalty is supposedly mandatory, use has been lacking. For example, recently, in Pittsburgh, Pennsylvania, a judge refused to invoke the additional penalty because he felt it jeopardized the criminal's right against double jeopardy.

The survey indicates that the mandatory additional penalty has, when applied, been assigned so that it will run concurrent with the penalty imposed for the other felony. When applied in this manner during sentencing of the criminal, the impact of the law is lessened. Taken together the total impact of additional mandatory sentences probably affects less than 10% of the total number of cases in which it should be applied.

Sportsmen and others who have supported this type of legislation have found it difficult to understand how our society can be so interested in protecting the criminal while it disarms the innocent citizen. They cannot understand how a permissive society thinks very little about protecting the individual citizen's constitutional rights and so much about protecting theman who willingly and knowingly violates the law and the public order.

Another way to state the same idea is this. If our society is unwilling to enforce laws already on the books, why create more laws? The average citizen can be expected to obey the laws which disarm him or which limit his exercise of his right. But the vital question is: would such laws actually reduce crime rates? If these laws will not so reduce crime rates measurably, it might well be that the legislatures are seeking the wrong solution to a pressing problem. It may be noted that such restrictive legislation has not protected the citizen in the states where such laws are now in effect.

A few months ago a well-known black militant was picked up by federal authorities for violating a 40-year-old law, a law which prohibits an individual under indictment for a crime of violence from carrying a firearm across states lines. The Washington *Post*, long a leading opponent of private ownership of firearms, and supporter of registration and even confiscation editorially supported the man in question, Rap Brown, and called the action of the FBI "discriminatory" and "incredible" and implied that the charge was trumped up. Put another way, a vocal agitator should have the right which the *Post* already in effect has denied to an average citizen. If this law is not to be enforced, what laws are to be enforced, and against whom?

If it is the misuse of firearms which society's wrath is to be directed against, then why would any rational legislator refuse to support legislation aimed only in that direction? And it is every bit as logically inconceivable that a judge charged with carrying out the law would fail to impose penalties provided in the law. The same stands true for those who are charged with prosecuting lawbreakers on behalf of society.

# CHAPTER 11

## THE COMMUNICATIONS MEDIA AND
## THE RIGHT TO BEAR ARMS

The team of Rowan and Martin arrived at the highlight of their comedy show, and the crowd in the studio awaited the weekly awarding of the "Flying Fickle Finger of Fate" plaque. The moment arrived, and who better to award it to than a well-known sportsman's association for teaching our children to learn how to shoot! A burst of laughter through the crowd. Success? Outlandish? Typical of newsmedia treatment of the right to keep and bear arms? Misplaced satire?

News reporter Harry K. Smith reported the tragic assassination attempt on the life of Presidential candidate George Wallace. Hardly had he left the subject of the assassination attempt itself than he launched into an irrational and irresponsible attack on firearms and called for registration of firearms. Certainly, Mr. Smith said, no legitimate sportsman could object to this harmless procedure. The innuendo was quite clear: registration would likely have prevented the attack on Governor Wallace. Serves Wallace right for taking a firm stand against "rational" firearms legislation.

The police raided the home of a suburban Washington, D.C. man and shot him, permanently disabling him. But as writers to the letters to the editor column in such respectable newspapers as the *National Observer* suggested that had the injured man not had guns to begin with the incident would never have happened. This theme was subsequently picked up in other news accounts of the aftermath of the tragedy.

A story purporting to meet the accepted TV standards for a nature story which told of a sportsman's hunt for polar bears actually used material from a tranquilizer expedition undertaken for scientific purposes. The sponsor of the program, Quaker Oats Company, was besieged with angry letters from sportsmen once the true facts were uncovered. The program had attempted to show that sportsmen needlessly and willfully slaughtered mother and baby animals.

Writing in the April 1, 1972, *TV Guide*, critic Cleveland Amory suggested that hunters were not worthy of rescue. He was reviewing the program *Emergency*, produced by Jack (*Dragnet*) Webb when he suggested

131

OUR VANISHING FREEDOM

that since the man in trouble in one episode was a hunter he was not worthy of the efforts of the show's heroes.

Recently Zack Mosely of the "Smilin' Jack" cartoon strip fame had one of his characters purchase a handgun out of state without any complication. In a column which has made its reputation on accurate reporting of the writer's concern, aircraft, this lapse of accuracy is certainly misleading and suggestive of revisions in laws regarding handgun purchases. Obviously this purchase was in violation of the 1968 firearms control act.

Chester Gould, creator of "Dick Tracy" recently suggested that firearms registration was both feasible and desirable. For a man whose criminals never have had any trouble getting firearms this is a curious position. More curious still is the suggestion that the major reason for such registration is the ease with which stolen firearms can be returned to their proper owners. As seen in treatment above, this simply does not happen very often.

In a questionnaire recently compiled by this writer, not one firearms authority could find a single instance of major support for the right to keep and bear arms in a single major magazine, television editorial, radio editorial or large city newspaper editorial. Further, this writer would like to receive documentation of such pro-gun stands if any do exist. The sportsman's journals and similar publications have of course taken pro-gun stands, and radio and TV stations have, under federal fairness rules, granted "equal time" to gun advocates in response to editorials originating in the stations themselves.

This becomes even stranger if one considers that most major polls conducted by/through the media have been pro-guns. The *Advocates* shows on public television reported a strong favorable response on the debate on the right to keep and bear arms. However, opponents suggested "bloc voting" by sportsmen which tended to invalidate the poll. After a search the producers suggested that to the best of their ability they have broken down voting patterns and still found about a 3 to 1 ratio favorable to the right to bear arms.

The flurry of pro-guns "letter to the editor" which invariably follow major anti-guns editorials again points out the displeasure of citizens (and readers) to these editorial policies. How many objections might be voiced to a pro-guns editorial has not been tested lately because of the refusal of the media to voice such sentiments.

The news media has been quite fair to the public in regard to the public's right to know when an event occurs which is negative vis a vis the right to keep and bear arms. Never let it be said that they fail to illustrate, publicize, or portray every incident of the misuse of firearms. The "Texas Tower" killings, the "Black Panther-Police Shootouts," and the murders of

132

police officers are given front page headlines. And so are fatal accidents, woundings and the like whether accidental or willful. A hold-up or hijacking involving a gun is always so reported. So are hunting accidents.

But what about the public's right to know about the good things which are done with firearms? Can we see television, press or radio coverage of National Matches, Olympic competition or other major shooting events? Publicity may be given to such events on smaller, local media, but seldom is there any interest in these events on the national level. Occasionally on *Wide World of Sports* there will be a short note taken of these events. And, despite the recent lessening of emphasis on hunting and shooting, there is the American Sportsman series.

The major national magazines, such as *Life*, have emphasized the racist overtones of some small percentage of gun owners and dealers. One infamous story in *Life* depicted a gun dealer who offered obsolescent military rifles with a "nigger back guarantee." Presumably this was a typical dealer. Major, modern, well-equipped and stocked sporting goods and gun dealers were for the most part ignored in the *Life* story. By analogy, one might wonder at Time-Life, Inc.'s possible reaction if one should use one of the various hate literature magazines as a primary example of the American press.

While, as noted previously, major city newspapers, such as the Washington *Post* and the New York *Times* have brought almost inordinate pressures on the Congress and their readers to pass restrictive firearms legislation, they have been only partially successful in their efforts. It has a given fact that large city newspapers will ipso facto be anti-guns. They have suggested, ironically, that organizations such as the National Rifle Association are lobbying groups when, if fact, they operate with far greater power and from a much stronger position that the N.R.A. could ever hope for. Put another way, a man might join the N.R.A. because he believes in the right to bear arms, and hence, is interested in all things pertaining to that interest. Conversely, one might subscribe to the *Times* for a wide variety of reasons, but most probably for its news coverage, which, hopefully, is somewhat objective. It is unlikely that he will subscribe because he favors restrictive firearms legislation. Yet almost daily for long periods many of these papers have flooded their columns with anti-firearms stories and editorials.

No one disputes the right of freedom of the press. Further, no one disputes the right to editorialize as a portion of that right. But editorials should be somehow objective, and, if not, should be for moral reasons clearly labeled as non-objective. Since a major newspaper consists of not one but many editorial writers occasionally an opposing view should be voiced if only to give credibility to the idea of a press free not only from governmental but other controls. In short, a great newspaper, journal or magazine does not need, and, in fact, cannot afford to lie and fabricate. Its very greatness should remove it from the type of brutal, misleading and disgusting attacks which have been characteristic of the assaults on the N.R.A. and other sportsman and outdoor organizations.

It would be possible to suggest that the very glorification of violence spawned by the media themselves is far and away more responsible for acts of violence than are guns. Ignoring for the moment the violence in radio, TV and comic strip programs, and concerning ourselves solely with news reporting, we find strong supporting evidence for this hypothesis. Inordinate attention seems to be given to mass or exotic murders and assassinations. The anti-hero of these stories is the architect of the crime. In-depth analyses of criminals is commonplace. Mired in obscurity these otherwise unimportant figures find that crime can vault them into the limelight of public pity, sympathy and interest. The vehicle for such interst is the news media.

To suggest that the newsmedia is itself responsible for crime is far too simplistic an explanation. Even to add violence in programming and stories and sob-sister pleas for sympathy for criminals in the media is not sufficient. But, to return to the point at hand, this explanation may be as significant as the media's image of the private ownership of weapons.

Television programming, while not a function of the news media per se is nevertheless a primary source of total political socialization. Additionally, it helps to mold public opinion, change attitudes and create value screens. It is far more subtle than news reporting and, in this way, potentially more dangerous. Images here are changed little by little with a great deal of entertainment and value-less viewing in between indoctrination sessions.

On ABC's *Owen Marshall* show recently (seen here 13 January 1972) the murderer "done it" with a mail-order weapon. Much is still made of this as a source of criminal guns as any frequent TV viewer can attest. Either the gun was obtained via mail intra-state or it was obtained before the 1968 gun law came into effect, for it is no longer possible to buy a gun this way in interstate commerce save between dealers. It is highly improbable that any dealer would risk the loss of license and criminal prosecution provided for in the 1968 law.

NBC's *Mystery Movie* (16 February 1972) had a gun dealer tell his most recent client that he would not go out on the streets with the people running around to whom he had sold guns. Most dealers of course make every reasonable attempt to obey the law which already prohibits sales to drug addicts, minors, habitual drunkards and the insane. Most dealers go beyond the bare requirements of the law, for a single sale does not mean that much a human life, a felony, etc., which could result from sales to the wrong people. No doubt mistakes are made, but no individual can predict all future actions of his customers. A car dealer cannot tell, for example, whether the car he sells will be used for crime or not. He exercises his best judgment and hopes that the law will restrain the criminal tendencies of his customer.

Automatic weapons appear frequently in the television crime stories. Yet automatic weapons have been under federal and state controls for nearly four decades. Additional restrictions were place on automatic and large bore weapons by the 1968 federal law. Whenever these weapons do appear they are in violation of existing laws.

A recent episode of *Adam-12* found police officers questioning the need of private citizens to own legal weapons for defense of their homes and places of business. In the story a gas station owner lost his large calibre revolver to a hold-up man who hitherto had had only a toy. Malloy had told him so. The criminal apprehended despite the added danger of the real weapon stolen from the victim turned out to be a white man who was impersonating a black man. After being stripped of his disguise the robber offered his opinion of "niggers." Malloy, playing one-upmanship, suggested that he was a kindred spirit to the victim of his felony. The remark presumably indicated that only a bigot would buy a pistol to defend himself. The facts of the situation are, of course, that every month hundreds of Americans defend their homes, property, families and selves using firearms. This is a basic right of Americans which we have covered extensively already.

With recent interests in ecology and the enviornment, hunters have been maligned consistently in movies and television programs. The hunter is the villian who seeks to kill the last egret, polar bear, whooping crane and/or bald eagle. No distinction is made between professional hunters who kill for bounty or on contract with a rancher on the one hand and the non-professional sportsman on the other hand. This is not to suggest that professional hunters are evil, but rather than, at times, these men will, for professional reasons, attempt to reduce or eliminate one or more species of animal from a given area. This is not true of sportsmen. The pros and cons of controlling or eliminating a given species in order for man to better or more economically utilize an area of land cannot be decided here. What is suggested is that there is a distinction to be made. Professional hunters *do* hunt, under contract, in national parks while sportsmen are not permitted to hunt. Sportsmen would use the carcass but not most professional hunters.

Various treatments of sportsmen in magazines, newspapers and journals as well as on television have not made this distinction. The wasteful sportsmen! But sportsmen voluntarily taxed themselves under the Pittman-Robertson Federal Aid in Wildlike Restoration Act to support the restoration of animals of all types, game and non-game. This tax money, over $450 million since 1937, has kept species near extinction in existence even when there is no hope of returning these species in quantities suitable for hunting. It is blatantly unfair to suggest that these projects are undertaken solely to provide targets for hunters.

The professional hunters of the old westerns who hunt down the last buffalo is completely out of date and inapplicable to the modern context. The average hunter attempts to kill older animals which can no longer reproduce in deference to the younger animals. Most sportsmen actively support restrictions on hunting, and, many times, have voluntarily reduced hunting seasons making them more restrictive than have the state legislators. Additional taxes, such as the 10% tax on handguns, have been supported by sportsmen when the monies are to be used for purposes of conservation.

There are reasons far beyond hunting for the demise of certain species of birds and animals. Destruction of breeding grounds, destruction of nests, pollution and other causes of death brought about by modern technology have taken substantial tolls. A clash of values between conservationists and technology may be the principal cause of the reduction of animal life.

In short, modern mass communications media have provided little in fairness and equity for the sportsman, the gun owner or the hunter. The gun enthusiast may have just cause for crying, "Foul!" at the media. The facts are ignored or distorted with such regularity that one can but speculate that there is no real interest in truth or fairness by any of the television networks, few major newspapers, few national magazines, few radio stations and few movie production companies. Little attention is paid to existing legislation in the writing of stories although the same media may call for even more restrictive legislation. In a word, the right hand does not know what the left is doing.

The lowest techniques of name-calling, innuendo and distortion or misrepresentation of fact have been called into play. And the game is played with one-sided rules. The media have available to them the awesome power of persuasion. It can be used day in and day out in a massive effort to sway legislative action. They have indicted the firearms industry, the sportsmen and shooters' associations and the honest citizen. They have charged guilt for murder and assassination, rape and robbery to the honest firearms-owning citizen while pitying the criminal and the assassin.

Perhaps if the same effort were utilized in more honest and rational ways a reduction in crime could be effected. Perhaps they cry out against guns because they feel a sense of guilt themselves. Perhaps they lack an historical sense and operate only at the pragmatic level. And perhaps they will effect restrictive legislation which, according to scientific research, will fail completely to control the situation for which their proposals are offered as a remedy.

# CHAPTER 12

## ADMINISTRATION AND THE LAW

As we teach American government to students in high schools and colleges, we say that the executive is to lead his nation or state and formulate legislation, the legislature is to examine prospective laws and then enact these, and the courts are to ensure the constitutionality of such laws. The function of the bureaucracy is to carry out these laws, generally under the direction of the executive office. Somehow we predicate a certain transparency to the bureaucracy in that we suppose, generally naively, that their efforts are pure. Never could a bureaucracy bring its own views to bear for the legislature has spelled out in great detail what the bureaucracy is to do, and that is that.

A bureaucracy does not operate in a vacuum. It is comprised of men and women who are subject to the same views, prejudices, politics and attitudes that affect all mankind. Some public servants are frustrated politicians who see their positions as one of influence from which they can frame the legislation which they believe will make the nation a Utopia. At times they find a legislative supporter who is quite willing to work on the same program. At other times they may work through one or more lobbies. They may also choose to go on extended speaking tours which are theoretically tied to their positions, but which are really disguised political activity. There is the unresolved question whether the bureaucracy should be permitted on its own initiative to draw up and initiate laws and then to give these publicity at the taxpayer's expense in public addresses, etc.

If the formulation of public policy by public servants is questionable, the willful disregard of legislative intent in the application of laws would certainly seem to be improper and illegal. Even the U.S. Supreme Court has held that laws which are, in and of themselves, constitutional may be rendered unconstitutional by misapplication through the bureaucratic process. The transition from constitutionality to unconstitutionality largely takes place in the issuance of rules and regulations by the agency concerned with the application of the law. In a hypothetical case, a legislature may allow a permit or license to be issued permissively by a bureaucratic agency, presuming that the agency will issue logical and reasonable standards to be used in assessing whether or not such permits or licenses will be issued in a given case. The bureaucracy in question may decide that it wishes no or very few highly selected permits or licenses to be issued. It may then issue few to none of these items. The legislature in making the law under which the bureaucracy operates probably had no set idea of the number of licenses or permits which might eventually be issued. However, the issuance of permits as allowed by law indicates that the legislature had the intention of permitting some.

The hardest legal question to decide in assessing the operations of a bureaucracy would be: how many is the "some" which the legislature intended to be issued. There are a number of possibilities to be considered. First, that the license or permit system is really a revenue-raising device and that the legislature intended that all applicants would be automatically granted the license or permit upon receipt of payment. Along the same line, the permit or license may be a means of gathering knowledge, in reality a form of registration. Second, the applications requested by the legislature may be a simple check on the applicants in order to bar issuance to certain classes of persons according to a rational pattern, e.g., handgun permits to convicted felons. Third, the legislature may wish to make its permit or license quite restrictive, based on some sort of examination and available only to a certain class of individuals, e.g., in administering medical practice certificates only to those completing medical school and passing an examination associated with the practice of this skill. Fourth, there is the possibility of rule by those within the bureaucracy. In such a case the intention of the legislature is ignored and the will of the bureaucracy reigns supreme.

If the latter be the case there are two possibilities. One is that the courts of the appropriate jurisdiction will find that the bureaucracy has overstepped its legitimate authority. The second possibility is that the legislature may also see that its will has been frustrated and take appropriate action. If we choose not to accept these two possibilities it is necessary to admit that a totalitarian situation exists unquieted. This situation is impossible in a republic, and goes beyond the immediate concern of this chapter.

The real problem lies in the circumstance that involves the individual. How indeed does the individual prove that the decision of the bureaucracy in his own case is arbitrary? In the case of New York's restrictive Sullivan Law, it would seem that the individual can find little protection for his own freedom. The New York case is worthy of note, for it had been clearly established that the petitioner was a master of arms, a veteran, and a man who had held a pistol permit for some considerable time without abusing that right. Only an arbitrary bureaucratic decision not to issue the permit prevented the petitioner from obtaining a renewal. Put in the opposite, the Court would likely have supported the issuing agent if it had chosen (arbitrarily) to have issued the permit. This strikes this writer as the epitome of arbitrary administration. To restate the case, it mattered not whether the permit was granted or not to the petitioner, despite the fact that the petitioner could, through its issuance, enjoy expanded freedom. Insofar as it is possible to predict human action, there was absolutely no reason to suspect that the petitioner would misuse his permit in the future. If this petitioner could not find relief in the New York court system, it would appear highly unlikely that any other single petitioner could expect to find relief either.

While it is true that the Congress chose to retract certain of the more recent anti-firearms legislation, it is nonetheless true that legislatures seldom retract offensive legislation. This is perhaps true in the large because the Courts have generally interceded when laws are offensive whether in design or in administration. One may once again choose to look at New York's Sullivan Law. The injustices not corrected by the courts are equally uncorrected by the legislature. Despite the obvious injustices and inequities in the issuance of permits, the Legislature has added additional restrictions in recent years. The inequities are obvious in the ease with which permits are issued in certain rural areas as contrasted with but a handful of permits issued annually in New York City.

When economic considerations are not of primary importance in legislation, it becomes even more difficult to have legislation repealed. A major failure of a program which is expensive in monetary terms may bring abandonment for a strict accounting can be had. However, a program which brings oppression of rights, especially if these persons are in a minority, may be more difficult to assess properly. The cost of alienation from rights enjoyed may be very high. For example, if the consumption of ramps, a noxious food native to West Virginia, were to be forbidden as food, this prohibition would affect a small minority of the citizenry to be sure. However, the denial of the right to consume ramps would be an unjust action of government. If such a law were to be enacted it might never be repealed, for it has no major economic effect, and it bears on only a tiny minority of the people.

Firearms legislation has simply and boldly failed to do what it was supposed to do. The purpose of restrictive legislation is to reduce crime and to insure peace in the streets. It is never easy to admit failure in a carefully prepared scheme which has been backed by passion and propaganda. It is nearly as difficult to alter the existing law and lessen its provisions. Instead, it has become normal to increase the intensity of legislation in hopes that increasingly more oppressive laws can do what less offensive one have failed to do. The blatant and widespread failure of alcohol prohibition had to be manifested over a considerable period of time before action was taken to repeal.

When an administrative agency is given charge of a new area of legislative mandate, it increases its size, its staff and its budget in order to meet the mandate. Should that area of legislative activity cease, the agency loses its power and its potential for power in these same vital areas. The span of control is increased, and former operatives become department heads, and the number of persons employed increases substantially. In a time of inactivity, these capacities cease as well. This can mean immediate loss not only of power, but of income as well, for the department head draws a much larger salary than does a mere operative agent. In short, a man's power and his income decreases as does the agency's operation in legislative cutbacks or court curtailment. The administrative agency thus has a vested interest in the continuation of the program in question.

Many administrators view stagnation as a sign of death. If an agency no longer grows in their view then it stagnates and death of the agency becomes a possibility. Thus the continued growth of power and functions within an agency becomes an administrative goal. This growth allows for greater specialization and for this agency to hire additional specialists. There are additional side-affects of growth. It is easier to hire a tenured incompetent in a larger organization. It allows for the operation of the so-called "Peter Principle" which permits an administrator to carry semi-competent or even incompetent favored subordinates up the administrative ladder with him. This administrative pork-barrel creates a strong inner ring of extremely loyal, if somewhat incompetent, subordinates who are devoted to the chief administrator. This, in turn, breeds increased irresponsibility, secrecy in policy formulation and adjudication, and even the possibility of insubordination to the legislators who created the agency.

The growth of research specialization increases the possibility of the agency lobbying for new legislation which will be designed to increase the agency's powers. The specialists may be engaged initially in studying the feedback process, i.e., in the studying of whether the agency is getting the job done. However, the same research team may quickly "discover" that the mission is failing because the Agency does not have quite

141

enough money or power or manpower or authority. The research teams then set themselves to proving this hypothesis. As so many recent studies have shown, the legislative branch of government is often even overwhelmed by the evidence garnered by the administrative agencies. Lacking staff, time, research facilities and assistants, the legislators tend to vote with the agency, for after all it is the one functionary of government which confronts the public daily in the operations of the law. They must then know their business. As legislative bodies are pressed for time and the legislators themselves grow weary, they often give in to the administrative desires simply to finish up the legislative session. The bureaucrats have outmaneuvered the elected representatives of the people and the will of the electorate.

This returns us to the point of origin. Given the fantastic workload of the legislative bodies, most notably of the Congress, it is not surprising that laws which are oppressive are seldom repealed by the legislative branch unless the oppression is so widespread and the failure of the program is so obvious that legislators, whether out of duty or out of fear of the electorate at the polls, simply must repeal that piece of legislation. In effect, the legislators generally have enough to do in each legislative session in new business alone to take up their time. Reconsideration of bills already in the code is generally out of the question. It is the administrative agencies who are to see to the bills after they are passed. The legislators generally see their work as completed when the bills are sent to the executive for his signature.

The executive office normally oversees the operations of the bureaucracy, which means that it oversees the way in which the legislation is carried out after it has been made part of the law of the land. However, the executive, especially the President of the United States, has become involved in a myriad of tasks, duties, functions, etc., and he seldom knows what is being done in the day to day operations of government. Herein lies the fallacy of large government. It takes on too many tasks and the elected representatives of the people, both in the executive and the legislative branches, cannot possibly oversee the operations of the functions properly.

If the executive seeks an explanation from his career administrators he can be sure that he will indeed be provided such information. It may come in volumes which must be then summarized and these summaries in turn further distilled into a brief presentation suitable for the executive. Even in the initial volumes, the clever administrator can conceal or mislead; it becomes even easier to do so in later summaries. The evidence submitted is culled carefully by experts, by administrators and by staff so that it presents a very interesting, if sometimes, misleading picture. The curious reader can find ample evidence in the Congressional Record, in the budget for the state or federal governments, in the reports of administrative bodies or even in their own yearbooks or press releases. Further, the testimony offered by most public bodies before legislative committees or other public or even private bodies makes interesting reading as well. Administrative experts backed by volumes of research and teams of skilled lawyers and others can baffle even the most dogmatic inquiry.

Many of the "blue ribbon" panels or other high level public commissions and bodies of inquiry have come to depend on the testimony, statistics and expert opinions of public servants. The questions asked by such committeemen are seldom answered directly or fully, unless this were to serve the purpose of the public servants. Statistics which might show, for example, that there is no correlation between gun control laws and crime rates might never be presented. While there may be times that such experts or bureaucrats may lie, this is not the point. The point is that seldom do administrative bodies present evidence which seems to be aimed at the curtailment of their functions, power, budgets or staff.

When public commissions are asked to weigh the opinions and testimony of public interest groups, lobbyists or private citizens against those of the public servants, the tendency is to trust the government itself. Presumably, those not associated with government step forward only when their "vested interests" are at stake. There seems to be a logical preference for government giving advice to government over the public advising government. The logic holds that the public bodies are seekers after truth and do not have vested interests to protect. As we have seen this is precisely the opposite of the truth. It is the considered opinion of this author that government generally has more at stake ("vested interests") than do private citizens.

It is then not surprising that many governmental reports find for the position of bureaucratic power. The bureaucracies have testified and have presented their opinions, their statistics, their experts and their version of the public interest. Because the legislators, at least at times, find that they have no vested interests at stake, these "impartial" findings become the opinions of the public commissions. This kind of prejudiced reporting adds to the feedback process. In effect, then, anything which a bureaucratic agency does to bring about its programs is seen as carrying out the public mandate. Their proof of a public mandate is found in the report of the commission which was fed the bureaucracy's conclusions.

Should the bureaucracy fail to have its designs incorporated into law they need not be fully frustrated. There are alternatives available, alternatives which may still allow for the introduction of bureaucratic rules. Since bureaucratic agencies are responsible for deciding the validity of many grant requests, they may tie the awarding of a grant to compliance with formal or informal guidelines which may be extra-legal. For example, the awarding of grant monies to local police training programs may be tied to a policy of local police taking a hard line in issuing permits to carry concealed weapons. If the local police should have jurisdiction over the issuance of permits to carry concealed weapons, those agencies which have become known as being highly restrictive may be given preference for federal monies which supplement local monies. As it becomes known that this is the policy of the granting agency at the federal level, those police departments wishing federal grant monies must at least consider seriously taking a more restrictive stand on the issuance of pistol permits if they wish to become eligible for money.

To prove that this is the formal policy of the bureaucratic agency becomes almost impossible, for most agencies having funds to award to local or state governments have far and away more requests than they can possibly fill. This is still true of the number of local or state agencies which meet the precise letter of the law, as incorporated in the bill funding the federal grant, i.e., that the number of possible recipients is much larger even if the total number is reduced by those marginally or partially ineligible.

If there is an inquiry about the denial of a grant request, the answer is readily available: Money is scarce. If the legislature had seen fit to provide more money then more awards could have been made. However, the line had to be drawn somewhere. Not all theoretically eligible requests could be honored. In short, not one word about the real reason, i.e., that the local or state police had a "liberal" firearms policy, needs to be spoken. If this happens the bureaucracy may triumph over the will of the legislature by imposing its own, additional and extra-legal requirements to the law of the land.

If it should become necessary to justify its actions, the bureaucracy can fabricate a fairly good response. The most obvious one is that there was an error somewhere in applications or supporting documentation. Given the growth of the size of applications and the required, additional supporting data, it is not surprising to find that many will indeed contain some error, whether large or small, important or unimportant, within its covers. When federal grants-in-aid programs began, a total grant request might have only been a dozen pages or less. Today few applications run under 200 pages. Many run into five or more bound volumes, including sociological data, crime statistics, payroll schedules, geographical surveys, etc.

If a more basic justification needs to be provided, the agency may find a justification which is perhaps even closer to the real truth. Since there are a number of applicants with nearly equal needs, then an inquiry into what the local or state government is doing for itself may be in order. If the aim is to reduce crime, and if the bureaucracy's prejudice lies in favor of firearms control, then "what the agency is doing for itself" might include a strong anti-gun law, if the grant is to be awarded, and no restrictive firearms legislation, if the grant is to be denied. In essence, the agency may be free by legislation, or may feel that it is free by desire, to draw up standards which can be used to create a ranking of applicants which will determine the order in which the awards will be granted. These standards will, of course, reflect the prejudices of the bureaucracy. In other words, the bureaucracy is thus able to create a set of arbitrary standards which must be met in order to receive an award and which are beyond the immediate control, and perhaps the immediate desires as well, of the legislature.

If the administrative agency chooses to involve itself with one or more commissions or groups, then it has immediate justification for the standards which it employs. Hence, if a public commission, perhaps using the agency's own experts, figures, data and other supporting materials, finds that gun control is an effective means of crime control, the agency has substantiated its standards. If additional data can be found in "public interest groups," "research groups," "study centers" or other foundation or educationally supported institution, this would seem to add additional justification to the agency's position. It is then not surprising to find these agencies giving much support to these friendly researchers. The support is seldom monetary, but the use of research facilities, interviews, research tools, data banks and the like can be even more valuable than money. There are no meaningful restrictions on the participation of public servants in educational or research institutions, especially on the public servant's own time, but also on his participation on government time. Participation in educational seminars is encouraged in most governmental agencies. One should not be surprised to find that these many times degenerate into political action indoctrination sessions. At the least, the policy of the administrative body will be defended with vigor.

Studies done on the political science professors invariably have shown that, in recent years, academia has leaned toward the political left. Most of the professors in the social sciences have tended to associate themselves with liberal or leftist causes in deference to the right or conservative politics. They will then be found to generally support the views of the liberal establishment, e.g., the *New York Times, Washington Post* or *New Republic*, or they support the leftist causes, e.g., *Ramparts*, S.D.S., or Progressive Labor, points of view. In the area of firearms control, most social and political scientists tend to follow the standard line of their associations. Despite a dip in the prestige of college professors during the era of student riots, many of which were led or inspired by the college teaching liberal establishment, the association of the considered opinions of learned scholars has done much to raise the prestige of the anti-firearms arguments. For example, we note here again the anti-gun article of Professor Hofstadter noted earlier in this book. Hence, these academic opinions, for seldom are the anti-firearms articles of the university origin researched thoroughly, can strengthen the position of the bureaucracy and its arbitrary standards.

What has just been said can also apply to many of the reports of private research groups, foundation supported research associations, centers for the study of political institutions and behavior, and the like. Many of these organizations support the liberal or leftist point of view. Others are apolitical, but are staffed by professional liberals, many of whom are anti-firearms in their own philosophy. Some are dependent upon governmental contracts or otherwise involved in the basic viewpoints of the bureaucracy, and hence simply turn out materials which reiterate, directly or indirectly, the established views.

The essential question of research done anywhere is: what are you trying to justify? Research is seldom valuable when it begins with a conclusion and then seeks to justify that position. Many times this is done irrespective of the evidence at hand. There are few, if any, positions which cannot be justified to some degree if there is enough time given to the research team. This does not mean that this is conclusive; it means simply that a body of theoretical knowledge, justified by some sort of data, can be built up for almost any social or political question. Information on a political question is often cyclic in argument, duplicated in interlocking documentation, and self-serving for the proponents of large government. As has been shown, such supporting information and argumentation can come from a wide variety of sources, but still rely on the same, highly selective documentation and sources, while ignoring, perhaps even totally, the other side of the question.

After the research has been accomplished, the next stage is the publicizing of the findings. Totalitarian governments have long depended upon internal propaganda to maintain regime support. Contrary to many popular images of support, most totalitarian governments have established a very high degree of loyalty by using the government's monopoly on information disemination. The old name of this technique, used so well by Adolf Hitler in nazi Germany, is "The Big Lie." If any statement is repeated often enough, it will, eventually, be believed by virtually everyone. One uses the churches, the radio or TV, newspaprs, public and private bodies, and so on, to get the same monolithic point of view across to the general population. Every modern totalitarian government since Hitler's Germany has successfully used this technique with success.

In a free and democratic government, there is supposed to be a free market place of ideas in which contending points of view can vie with one another for public support. The government's use of propaganda is offensive to the freeman. All points of view are to contend without special treatment to one point of view. Milton saw the necessity of this in his classic defense of free speech, when he wrote of Truth, "Let her and falsehood grapple, for never was it known that Trust was put to the worse." The question here is whether the defense of the right of the free people to keep and bear arms has been "put to the worse" because of the failure of our system to allow for the defense of this right. As we have seen, the news media, the communications media, and the larger news-papers and magazines are almost universal in their condemnation of this right. The proponents of the right are depicted as undesirables of every type. In effect, they seem not to be able to either respect or understand that another point of view may be stated without ridicule or attack. Some of the anti-firearms propaganda, notably of the big city papers, depicts firearms owners as fascists, Hitlerites or totalitarians, which seems ironic when one considers that firearms owners have not used the totali-tarian technique of attempting to silence their opponents' points of view.

Even if the private sector of the market place, wherein ideas are to compete, fails, this in no way justifies the involvement of government in the distribution of internal propaganda. In fact, quite the contrary is true; government should remain far outside the somewhat one-sided controversy so that at least some sort of free dialogue can still exist. And this is the point here. Our question is: Has government added to the already over-balanced situation by involving itself on the side of the underpublicized? If by "government" here we speak largely of the actions of the bureauc-racy, and if these people sense that the time is at hand that, by involving themselves to some degree, they can tip the scales enough to get the desired anti-firearms legislation, this involvement is not really surprising. The point is whether such involvement is a legitimate operation of publicly paid bureaucrats.

Many bureaucrats find that one way to become involved in politics is to accept speaking engagements before friendly and sympathetic audiences. This brings in support from a part of the general public for the work being carried on by the agency. Such a speech gives the opportunity to justify, most often without fear of contradiction, the agency's operations. A typical speech would contain a listing of the work done by the agency, an explanation of its beneficial results which are enjoyed by the average, law-abiding citizen, and a series of attacks on those who would dare to call these operations into question. In the latter portion of the speech, the bureaucrat will create the proverbial straw man, by stating the most simplistic objections in an unfavorable light, and then answering methodically each of the insignificant objections. If one were to see the counter-arguments which are reportedly used by the opponents of bureaucratic action he would almost necessarily tend to support the public servant's contention that these are ridiculous.

Even more objectionable still are the hints given by the public servant that there are myriads of good things which are still to be done by the agency if only they had more power. The bureaucrat hints that his agency is on the threshold of a major breakthrough, but these efforts have been frustrated by a handful of persons who are seeking private gains. There are generally the same persons already decimated by the bureaucrat's logic in the "straw man game." Some men are even more bold in their suggestions for improving their services. Mr. Serr of the AFTD of the Internal Revenue Service was engaged for some time in a public relations tour for additional firearms legislation several years ago. There was some considerable negative feedback on Mr. Serr's tour, for it appeared to some that he had overstepped the legitimate boundaries of bureaucratic involvement in politics.

There are good reasons to object to the self-serving involvement of the bureaucracy in the process of making laws. The bureaucracy is not responsible directly to the general public. They are not the elected representatives of the population. Their involvement in politics during the time when they are being paid to serve the whole public is the same as the governmental funding of propaganda agencies. It is in essence public funding of political statements, opinions and positions.

The ethics of public involvement in politics at the taxpayer's expense is underdeveloped. While bureaucratic agencies may need public relations departments for some, few legitimate uses, the unbridled involvement of bureaucracies in politics is dangerous to the freedom of the American people. How far should the bureaucracies be permitted to go? Are the advertisements created by the Social Security people really ethical? There are those who legitimately hold rational views that, in fact, social security is not as good as reported by the involved agency. The reader may recall the major effort made in the late 1940's and early 1950's, especially on television, to erase the negative image of bureaucrats. Is it the proper job of a republican government to prepare and distribute propaganda aimed at upgrading its images? At what point in this process does the political scientist or the moral philosopher draw the line between what is legitimate propaganda efforts by the government and what is essentially totalitarian?

If a Congressman questions a bureaucratic representative in an open hearing concerning what legislation action should be taken in order to upgrade the agency's programs or services, he is certainly under an obligation to give his opinion. But does the same bureaucrat have the ethical right to write to a Congressman, giving his unsolicited opinions on what is needed in his opinion? Does the bureaucrat have the right to write new control programs into his prospective program budget without direct authorization from the executive to do so? Does the bureaucrat have the right to open the door at legislative hearings to prospective programs he wishes to have aired by the legislators? We are not suggesting here that the answers to any or all of these questions be negative. We are suggesting that these are questions which should be asked in determining the framework within which we should create a strict ethical code for bureaucracies. Once adopted, this code should be strictly enforced. When framing the law, particular attention should be paid to the maintenance of a free and republican form of government as opposed to a totalitarian propaganda machine.

Even if the bureaucracy is checked in any attempt which it might make to establish restrictive rules on firearms through the manipulation of grant money, this in no way precludes such action by the legislature. Throughout the history of the legislative process in the United States there have been unfortunate compromises which have resulted in the loss of freedom. It happens in the following manner. Let us say that political conservatives wish to fund additional training for law enforcement officers. The liberals oppose this action, but wish to restrict private ownership of firearms. One member suggests that a compromise can be reached by funding police training programs provided that the states pass restrictive legislation on firearms ownership by the general public. Thus there is something in the bill for both sides. The liberals are assured of restrictions on firearms ownership while the conservatives receive their funding support for their scheme. While this may be a slight overstatement of a potential compromise, nevertheless by such omnibus bills are such deadlocks resolved.

If such a compromise as is suggested here were to be offered, the compliance with the obligations which is necessary for funding for police

149

training programs would be voluntary. If a state wished to protect the rights of its citizens to keep and bear arms it could do so. The price however would be support from the federal government for that state's police training programs. The state would then have to fund its own programs if any were to exist. Some would regard this kind of compromise as illegitimate, but it is certainly a part of the formal legislative process in the United States.

There are many precedents for using federal monetary powers to force states to perform in certain ways desired by the Congress. The federal government has withheld monies under matching grant programs for non-compliance with federal guidelines in such diverse policy areas as education, minority hiring practices, standards for road building, racial integration of many institutions, and voting standards. Without ever voting on a federal firearms law, and without dealing directly with the prohibitions in the Second Amendment to the Constitution, the federal government could, by manipulation of federal funding of state programs, force the states into adopting restrictive firearms legislation. Should the federal court system fail to "incorporate" the second amendment under the 14th amendment, thus applying it to the states, the federal government could circumvent the Constitution and restrict the rights of the citizens of the United States.

The Congress could simply tie additional monies in certain areas of grants subsidies to the requirement that the states take certain actions to reduce crime, without ever mentioning firearms restrictions. The Congress, by the individual efforts of several of its members, could indicate that clearly implied in these orders is the "legislative intent" that these measures should include restrictive firearms legislation. The bureaucracy would then be free to draw up its standards which would then include restrictive firearms legislation. A blank grant of power to the bureaucracy to "draw up standards" for crime control could imply more than sufficient power to include similar regulations.

In the final analysis, there are many means which the federal government can employ to circumvent the intention of the Founding Fathers in the Second Amendment. The final determination of the validity of these means will have to be made by the federal courts. It is to be hoped that the courts will, one day soon, choose to interpret the Second Amendment. When this case is heard, it is further hoped that the courts will do better than did the Supreme Court of New Jersey when it cited the curious volume by Mr. Bakal, reviewed above. Until this sort of judicial interpretation is available, one may suggest that the bureaucracy and the Congress should operate under the rather favorable pro-firearms divisions in the past. However, this restraint is very unlikely.

150

# INDEX

OUR VANISHING FREEDOM

OUR VANISHING FREEDOM

Washington, Lawrence, n.6
Webb, Jack, n.135
Whiskey Rebellion, 10
Wide World of Sports, 137
William and Mary (English monarchs), 4
World Council of Churches, 98
Wright, Quincy, 5

# INDEX OF COURT CASES